Advance praise for
VOICE OF THE PEOPLE

"If the shrill partisan rhetoric of American politics has become poisonous, then this book is the best antidote. Read it and weep for what America has lost; then read it again and celebrate for what we can find – if only we heed this book's timely advice."

MARK GERZON, *Author*
"Leading Through Conflict: How Successful Leaders Transform Differences Into Opportunities"

"*Voice of the People* is a pragmatic invitation to all Americans, regardless of political persuasion, to work together as citizens to solve the great challenges we face that transcend the current partisan divides. Turner and Chickering are essentially proposing that those of us who care about our country and the common good must see ourselves as the new transpartisans, beyond left and right, who can break this political stalemate."

– BOB EDGAR
President, Common Cause

"The transpartisan movement has begun to move America beyond the stale partisan rhetoric and fixed bayonets of past arguments. There are ways to rephrase questions and look anew at old challenges that unite Americans more than they divide us. *Voice of the People* highlights many of these new ways of looking at old challenges."

– GROVER NORQUIST, *conservative activist and President, Americans for Tax Reform*

Read more **Voice** c
reviews starting c

Also by A. LAWRENCE CHICKERING

Strategic Foreign Assistance:
Civil Society in International Security
(co-authored with Isobel Coleman, P. Edward Haley, & Emily Vargas-Baron)

Beyond Left and Right:
Breaking the Political Stalemate

The Silent Revolution:
The Informal Sector in Five Asian and Near Eastern Countries
(co-edited with Mohammad Salahdine)

Public Employee Unions:
The Crisis in Public Sector Labor Relations (edited)

The Politics of Planning:
A Review and Critique of Centralized Economic Planning (edited)

Also by JAMES S. TURNER

The Chemical Feast: The Nader Report on
Food Protection at the U.S. Food and Drug Administration

Making Your Own Baby Food:
An Exposé of the Baby Food Industry with Recipes
(co-authored with Mary Dustan Turner)

Protest! Student Activism in America - Edited by Foster and Long
Chapter "Student Power, Free Speech at Ohio State"

Issues & Trends In Health - by Carlson and Newman
Chapter "Controlling the Chemical Feast: How to Survive the
Expanding Crisis in Food Safety"

The Environmental Handbook - Ballantine/Friends of the Earth Book
Chapter "On How To Be A Constructive Nuisance" - Harrison Wellford,
with John Esposito, and James Turner

Encyclopedia of the Consumer Movement
Entry on the Food and Drug Administration,
co-author with Alexander Grant

Encyclopedia of the Future
Entry on The Future of Consumerism

VOICE OF THE PEOPLE:

THE
TRANSPARTISAN IMPERATIVE
IN AMERICAN LIFE

by

A. LAWRENCE CHICKERING

and

JAMES S. TURNER

Preface by STEPHEN P. COHEN, Founder and President
Institute for Middle East Peace and Development

daVinci Press

Requests for permission to reproduce selections
from this book should be addressed to:

da Vinci Press
7127 Hollister Avenue, Suite 8
Goleta, California 93117

www.davinci-society.org

LIBRARY OF CONGRESS
CATALOGING-IN-PUBLICATION DATA

CHICKERING, A. LAWRENCE
TURNER, JAMES S.

VOICE OF THE PEOPLE: The Transpartisan Imperative in American Life

ISBN 978-0-615-21526-6

1. American Politics   2. Political Philosophy

The da Vinci Society was founded by a group primarily of Silicon Valley
entrepreneurs to develop, test, and publicize innovative, "human scale"
solutions to major global issues. Following our goal to publish books
and monographs promoting public debate, we have chosen a radical
new book on American politics, co-authored by a "conservative" and a
"liberal" as our first publication.

Published in the United States by
da Vinci Press

Composition by
CASTEEL GRAPHIC DESIGN

Printed in the
United States of America

Dedication

To the next president of the United States, whether John McCain or Barack Obama, and the 130 million or more transpartisans, about whom we have written. Working together, they will give America a new birth of freedom, ensuring that "government of the people, by the people, for the people, shall not perish from the earth."

Contents

Foreword

The da Vinci Society was founded by a group primarily of Silicon Valley entrepreneurs to develop, test, and publicize innovative, "human scale" solutions to major global issues. We believe that *people* are the major underutilized resources onissues ranging from reform of public schools to promoting democracy in developing countries. We believe that the potential of individuals to contribute is often left out of the large visions that governments, international organizations, and large private organizations have for promoting global change.

Following our goal to publish books and monographs promoting public debate, we have chosen a radical new book on American politics, co-authored by a "conservative" and a "liberal" as our first publication. The authors have come together to present a "transpartisan" vision of our politics that seeks to unite and empower people across all loyalties by focusing on those areas where people can agree as much as or more than on those where they disagree.

Voice of the People: The Transpartisan Imperative in American Life, by A. Lawrence Chickering and James S. Turner, presents a powerful critique of America's current political system. The authors emphasize the value of strong commitment to citizen engagement in solving problems ranging from the crisis in public education, to the continuing challenge of race, to major issues related to foreign policy and national security. They challenge us to think about these and other issues in new ways that will help end the alienation many voters now feel toward the political system.

Highlighting the role of citizens in solving public challenges brings to mind the many "unsung heroes" who have been leading the way without significant recognition. We have selected one such hero to write the preface for this book. He is Stephen P. Cohen, a Harvard-trained social psychologist who has exemplified transpartisan values in his career of three decades focusing on reducing conflict in the Middle East — a career for which he deserves widespread recognition. We are pleased to have someone of Dr. Cohen's stature writing the preface for this important book.

The Society's first book is being published by our subsidiary, da Vinci Press. Other publications are being developed, presenting transpartisan analyses of other major issues. These include: a view from "inside" the challenges of reforming public schools; an analysis of the new challenges facing foreign policy; the dilemma of the new, "weak" states that have become the principal threats to international security; a presentation of transpartisan capitalism; and a new, path-breaking, transpartisan study of race in America.

To promote public debate on these issues, we are entering into a strategic alliance with two national organizations: the Washington, DC-based "Transpartisan Center"; and "Democracy in America," based in Ashland, Oregon. The founders of these organizations have worked over the past four years to bring together engaged conservatives, liberals and independents interested in exploring transpartisan strategies for addressing major public issues. This triple alliance will sponsor regular "salons" in Washington, DC, and elsewhere.[1]

LARRY BIEHL, Founder
The da Vinci Society

Preface

I have spent my entire professional life trying to help people bring peace to arguably the world's most dangerous place: the Middle East. The central challenge is getting people to look ahead and see future possibilities – to the futures of their children and grandchildren – and escape the tragedies of the past. The key to success is creating trust among people in conflict, people unconnected in normal life. The lesson from the Middle East is clear: there can be no peace without trust and no trust without peace and both trust and peace require personal subjective contact among individual people of strong competing loyalties.

The key to trust is doing things together. It is engaging people in common purposes. When people come together in real engagement, their conflicts and differences start to melt away – sometimes very quickly.

The Voice of the People: The Transpartisan Imperative in American Life applies these lessons to America's troubled political system. The authors address the acute conflict in American politics and the widespread alienation that Americans feel from their political system. They advocate expanding the vision of "public" beyond government to people. They argue for a new kind of politics, one that brings people together and encourages citizens to play a greatly increased role in public spaces. It would be a politics based on human engagement and trust, both at high policy levels and in communities across the country.

The authors propose solutions based on real examples of "transpartisan" success, in which citizens have organized and partnered with governments to solve problems ranging from public school reform, to racial tension, to major issues of national security and foreign policy.

They advocate a strong, empowered concept of citizenship, which encourages us to think in new ways about many public issues. Powerful examples exisit of their vision in action, and empowering citizens to form strong citizen organizations to play this new transpartisan role should greatly reduce alienation and increase support for the U.S. political system and its leaders.

The authors cite examples of successful transpartisan action from all parts of the world — educational reform in India, prison reform in California, healthcare initiatives in Denmark, and social entrepreneurship in South Africa, among many other examples. These successes need to be exposed to the world, talked about, and adapted to fit the needs of all the world's peoples facing similar challenges. We can often agree on the results we want; but we need to learn from one another how to achieve them. We can truly build upon each other's progress.

This is the promise of the transpartisan way. It is time the *Voice of the People* be heard.

STEPHEN P. COHEN
Teaneck, New Jersey
May 2008

vox populi, vox Dei
"The voice of the people, the voice of God"

19TH CENTURY AMERICAN
POPULIST POLITICAL SLOGAN

Introduction and Overview

In 1990, during the more hopeful times after the end of the Cold War, Nobel Laureate V.S. Naipaul placed the United States of America at the fulcrum of world progress. In an essay titled "Our Universal Civilization" he wrote:

> This idea of the pursuit of happiness is at the heart of the attractiveness of the universal civilization to so many outside it or on its periphery. ... I don't imagine my father's Hindu parents would have been able to understand the idea. So much is contained in it; the idea of the individual, responsibility, choice, the life of the intellect, the idea of vocation and perfectibility and achievement. It is an immense human idea. It cannot be reduced to a fixed system. It cannot generate fanaticism. But it is known to exist, and because of that, other more rigid systems in the end blow away.

Today, less than two decades later, our world is consumed by fears:

- Fears of violent terrorism
- Fears of chemical, biological, and nuclear weapons
- Fears of global destruction wrought from environmental imbalance
- Fears of pandemic disease and death by poverty, ignorance and doubt

War, famine, plague and death once again ride toward the Apocalypse.

Under this implacable assault, the values of a universal civilization seem tentative, fragile and dangerously vulnerable. At the same time, America seems to have lost its footing as a world leader and is conflicted over what to do and how to do it. It is widely believed that this conflict is caused by deep cultural divides within American society.

As a "conservative" (Chickering) and a "liberal" (Turner), we see the world very differently from those proclaiming a divided America. We believe there is little evidence of cultural conflict. We see the combat in our politics as:

- More a result of the *structure* of our political institutions than an expression of cultural division,

- More encoded into the nature of our political *debate* than an expression of our political *beliefs*, and

- More inflamed by a mass media addiction to conflict than by real differences among actual individuals.

A perfect example of Washington's addiction to conflict was expressed by a young conservative activist recently, in responding to news that one of us (Chickering) is working on a program that promotes education for girls in India. He responded dismissively and without hesitation, "Well, *nobody* is against *that!*" His meaning was clear. No one could bother being *for it* either.

Washington Post ombudsman Deborah Howell reported another example. She wrote on June 15 2008, that the paper did not cover the celebration of Israeli independence held on the Washington mall because it "was listed on a story budget to cover only if a conflict occurred." No conflict occurred Howell makes one of our key points saying "Conflict is not the only thing that is newsworthy." We go even farther saying that often a *lack* of conflict *is* the story.

We believe that many, if not most, Americans today feel a deep unhappiness over a political system that no longer serves the great majority of the people. We believe that most Americans are more aligned with traditional American values than the media reports, and are more alienated from contemporary American politics than political leaders acknowledge.

We look around the country and the world, and we see manifold examples of cooperation — people working together without significant conflict. Such cooperative interaction we call "transpartisan" — focusing on what unites us rather than what separates us. "Transpartisan" action focuses on understanding issues in new ways and creates spaces for cooperation that are sadly often hidden.[1]

It is important to distinguish "transpartisan" from "bipartisan". "Bipartisan" action is compromising: reducing conflict by splitting the difference. While this may, at times, be useful, it is not, in our view, sufficient. "Transpartisan" includes "bipartisan" but also goes beyond it. Transpartisan typically involves looking at an issue in a new way that will bring apparent adversaries together. The central transpartisan insight has to do with broadening the meaning of "public" beyond governments to include citizens engaging each other often in informal partnerships with governments to solve public problems.

Transpartisanship can also operate at high policymaking levels when one side backs off from its advocacy of a position, letting the other side come in and unite the political culture in favor of a new vision or approach. Nixon going to China is the archetypal example of this, but there are many others. This pattern is especially important in our discussion of the paradoxical logic of major policy reforms (see Chapter 11).

Transpartisan solutions, which promote collaboration, succeed by drawing on both conservative and liberal traditions and the values of each that are woven into the fabric of American culture. The conservative values that are most important to the transpartisan vision are individualism, entrepreneurship, and decentralized authority. Conservatives believe that transformative potential can most powerfully be realized through connected, individual and community, initiatives. The liberal values we would add to the transpartisan dynamic include individualism, special concern for the disadvantaged, equality of opportunity, equality of result understood in how people engage each other, and commitment to associations and connections that reach beyond the homogenous qualities of class, race, gender, religion, etc.

The transpartisan vision seeks to combine *conservative means* with *liberal ends*. It can avoid the convulsive, mechanical changes that are so common in conventional public policy-making by employing more incremental, organic strategies that avoid the sudden change that so often engenders fear and results in opposition and subversion.

Transpartisan connects all of these values by promoting a *strong concept of citizenship*. This concept has been, consciously or unconsciously, emasculated by the institutions and policies of both conservative and liberal governments.

Both conservatives and liberals are today crippled by their preoccupation with *governments* while ignoring the role that active *citizens* can play in helping solve public problems. This preoccupation with governments often produces lifeless institutions devoid of the human engagement and contact that are crucial to a society that deserves to be called "humane and just." Our goal is to bring people together from both sides — citizens inside the government and outside — to engage each other in ways that maximize their respective contributions in solving public challenges.

We will argue that by

1. Understanding issues in new ways,

2. Bringing together powerful strains of both conservative and liberal thought, and

3. Empowering citizens and communities,

people will come together to help solve problems that otherwise seem beyond solution. We think this is important. If we could only do more with what we agree upon, and spend less time fighting about our disagreements, we could achieve economic, social and political progress that now seems beyond our reach. We see this essay as focusing and fueling an ongoing conversation and invite all its readers to join this discourse. Transpartisanism is a community activity with a place for all interested parties.

Our vision of an engaged and *living* society is powerful, not only in its simple appeal to values that people know privately are true but also as demonstrated by a wide range of experiences in social transformation happening in all regions of the world. Our values and institutions, as defined by the Declaration of Independence, the Constitution, and the Bill of Rights, and our citizens are strong and perfectly suited to confront the challenges before us.

Has America lost its capacity for leadership?

We think not. Being transpartisan offers a way to lead.

Part I

The Crisis in Our Politics: Partisan Fatigue

Today's politicians disgust Americans. Before the 2006 elections, *Time Magazine* reported that a mere thirty-nine percent of likely voters approved of the Republican Congress. Forty-nine percent disapproved. At the same time, Congressional Democrats hovered at a thirty-nine percent approval rating, with fifty-six percent believing Democrats offered no clear set of alternative policies. On April 2, 2007, the Associated Press reported approval ratings of the new Democratic Congress at forty percent, with disapproval at fifty-seven percent.[1] The same day President Bush fared worse, with a thirty-five percent approval and sixty-seven percent disapproval rating.[2] These numbers continue to drop.

Americans disdain partisanship, as evidenced by the examples below.

Judy at AOL urges a unity campaign to fight both major parties, so that everyday people have more influence "than rich lobbyists, the media, and a handful of voters in early primary states."[3]

A Bluefield, West Virginia, man joins Judy saying, "I believe the constant fighting, bickering, and personal vendettas by both parties in Washington are detrimental to the welfare and national security of this country... I don't think any of the incumbents deserve reelection. Let's clean house and get a fresh start."[4]

From Washington State Phil says, "People don't talk politics anymore, except with people they agree with. You don't talk about it in the café. There's just the hate letters in the papers. It wasn't always that way. The language of the campaigns has escalated in a way that has sort of brought out the worst in people. It's really divided communities — and families."[5]

Despite people's antagonism toward conflict and partisanship, many Americans feel caught in a political system overwhelmed by conflict. They respond to the picture painted by Pulitzer Prize-winning journalist David Broder after the 2000 presidential election. "The divide went deeper than politics. It reached into the nation's psyche. The election left exactly half the country excited and optimistic and the other half concerned or scared."[6] The electronic media drove this sense of divide home on election nights in 2000 and 2004 with powerful graphic statements showing national maps of the country divided into red states and blue states ("conservative" and "liberal").[7]

Today, both left and right seize on the widespread conception of deep political and cultural conflict, pitting the majority of Americans against asserted elites who they describe as hostile to traditional American values. Conservatives say the left-leaning media, entertainment industry, celebrities and other cultural elites are undermining society's moral fiber by preaching "sex, drugs, rock and roll" and other such dead doctrines of the permissive 1960s. Liberals say financial elites manipulate government, the media and consumers so as to amass personal fortunes that they use to undermine middle class viability, destroy the economic well-being of families and communities, and cripple what is necessary to sustain traditional democratic values.

Despite widespread belief to the contrary, however, there is no evidence of any deep partisan divide poisoning American institutions and political discourse, neither in our past history nor in the present. The problem lies in the terms of the debate. We need to rethink multiple issues, discover new possibilities that will bring people together, and create new hope to solve issues that are now thought to be beyond solution.

CHAPTER ONE

WHAT 'DIVIDE'?: OUR PHANTOM POLITICAL CONFLICTS

Although the evidence shows that our country does suffer deep political and cultural divisions, the conflicts are not among ordinary people; they are between ordinary people and political elites. In our highly stylized political structure, everyone, winners and opponents alike, play dehumanizing roles that cause the whole apparatus to resemble a cross between sumo wrestling and Kabuki theatre.

Elites, winners and opposition both, exaggerate and promote conflict primarily by focusing all their attention on governments for solutions. They ignore the powerful opportunities for citizens to play active, connected, and critical roles — roles that often require partnering with governments. Simultaneously, citizen constituents play the role of impotents, opting out of voting, disillusioned with governing elites, and drifting out of political activity. Nothing can be done, they seem to say; the system is stacked against us.

At the same time they feel alienated from the political system, ordinary citizens are increasingly empowered by affluence, technology, and other factors to play a more active role, and they are demanding it. This increases the conflict.

Our leaders appear at odds with the very people they claim to represent. Our citizens challenge them and our political institutions in ways for which neither is well prepared, for two reasons:

1) American culture in the twenty first century has grown big, varied, and vibrant, and

2) Citizens have become active and connected, primarily by technology, transportation, and affluence, as never before.

Demographic trends, the emerging information culture, and the power of historical American imperatives are creating a new political constituency, one that offers a powerful, new role for citizens in public spaces and a new hope for solving problems that in the past have seemed beyond solution. This powerful, new popular force explains, in part, the results of the presidential primary contests for both the Democratic and Republican Parties in 2008. As of this writing, the anti-establishment (though we would say not yet transpartisan) candidates, McCain and Obama, seem to have overcome the organizational and political pressures of the Establishment — represented by the Clintons for the Democrats and by the "conservatives" for the Republicans. This new, transpartisan force has been, until now, excluded from mainstream politics by a combination of economic, institutional, and philosophical factors that have promoted conflict while concealing opportunities for collaboration. But now the transpartisans are the majority of Americans; as this majority engages, things will change.

The Divided America Myth

Morris P. Fiorina, senior fellow at the Hoover Institution and professor of Political Science at Stanford, in a book called *Culture War: The Myth of a Polarized America*, states the reality:[1] "[T]here is no culture war in the United States — no battle for the soul of America rages, at least none that most Americans are aware of." "The myth of a culture war," he writes,

> rests on misinterpretation of election returns, a lack of comprehensive examination of public opinion data, systematic and self-serving misrepresentation by issue activists, and selective coverage by an uncritical media more concerned with news value than with getting the story right. There is little evidence that Americans' ideological or policy positions are more polarized today than they were two or three decades ago, although their choices often seem to be.

Fiorina states the key distinction: "The explanation is that the political figures Americans evaluate are more polarized. A polarized political class makes the citizenry appear polarized, but is it largely that – an appearance." On most issues, he writes, "America is not the fatally polarized nation we often imagine it to be. On most issues, the majority of red-staters and blue-staters are on the same side." He includes the following examples:

> Upward of 35 percent of gun owners voted for John Kerry in 2004, as did a similar proportion of born-again Christians. A narrow majority of red-state residents joined a larger majority of blue-state residents who favored making gun regulations stricter. Solid majorities of blue-state residents share red-state residents' support for the death penalty and opposition to gay marriage. Political differences? Yes. A cultural chasm? No.

Fiorina cites research of political scientists Christopher R. Ellis and James A. Stimson "that only one-fifth of self-classified conservatives held consistently conservative views on both social and economic issues. About one-third were consistent social but not economic conservatives, and about one-sixth were consistent economic but not social conservatives. One-third of self-classified conservatives were neither consistent social nor economic conservatives on specific issues."

On abortion he reports that about thirty percent of self-identified Democrats believe that abortion should be "legal under all circumstances" and only about thirty percent of Republicans believe abortion should be "illegal in all circumstances." Large pluralities of both parties prefer "legal only under certain circumstances." He reports the 2004 National Election Study, finding that twenty-three percent of Americans who classified themselves as strong Republicans said that abortion should always be legal, compared to twenty-two percent who said that it should never be legal.

In 2005 Jonathan Rauch, writer-in-residence at The Brookings Institution, elaborated on these themes, after surveying polling and research data on the American electorate:

> In a two-party universe, things indeed now look impassionedly divided and inflamed. But, we do not live in a two-party universe. The fastest-growing group in American politics is independents, many of them centrists who identify with neither party and can tip the balance in close elections. According to the Pew Research Center for the People and the Press, since the Iraq War thirty percent of Americans have identified themselves as Republicans, thirty-one percent as Democrats, and thirty-nine percent as independents (or "other"). Registered voters split into even thirds.[2]

The 2005 Pew study elaborates:

> The typology study's finding of significant cleavages within parties not only runs counter to the widespread impression of a nation increasingly divided into two unified camps, but also raises questions about political alignments in the future. In particular, the study suggests that if the political agenda turns away from issues of defense and security, prospects for party unity could weaken significantly. ... [N]umerous opportunities exist for building coalitions across party lines on many issues currently facing the nation... coalitions that, in many cases, include some strange political bedfellows. Overall, there are many more shades to the American political landscape than just the red and blue dividing the Electoral College maps last November 2nd.[3]

The Pew data showed that on issues of the environment, immigration, government regulation, and isolationism versus global activism, major fissures exist in one or both political parties. (The contentious immigration debate within the Republican Party may be merely a precursor of more contention to come on more issues within both parties.)

The Pew data also showed divides both between and within the major parties on six issues – religion and moral values, welfare, cooperation with allies, business and free markets, cynicism about politics, and individualism versus federalism. Today, three years after the Pew study, even "national security" no longer serves as a clear demarcation between "conservatives" and "liberals."

On real issues, "red" and "blue" partisan posturing fails to define the multihued civic discourse underway across the country. Pew drew its data from voters identified as major party partisans – the party stalwarts. It addressed only tangentially the Americans who fail to identify with either of the two major parties. When the values and views of these unaffiliated Americans are considered, there is even more American unity than the Pew study found.

Even on an ostensibly contentious issue like immigration majorities, more than sixty percent – including sixty-six percent of Republicans and seventy-two percent of Democrats - who support creation of a guest-worker program also support broad provisions of the immigration bill that failed the US Senate amidst partisan bickering.[4] Sixty-one percent believe that we should have stayed out of Iraq, and sixty-three percent believe we should withdraw by 2008. Today, seventy-two percent of Americans – more than at any other time since the *Times/CBS News* poll began asking the question in 1983, agree that "generally things in the country are seriously off on the wrong track".[5]

While partisans may populate the extremes, ordinary people mix and match values from allegedly competing menus. Rauch quoted sociologist and opinion researcher Alan Wolfe, saying he "found his subjects to be 'above all moderate,' 'reluctant to pass judgment,' and 'tolerant to a fault.' Because opinion polls are designed to elicit and categorize disagreements, he concluded, they tend to obscure and even distort the reality of agreement."[6]

Rauch puts all the data together to answer the core question he poses: is there a chasm dividing America? "In the fifty-fifty nation," he asks, "does the distribution of opinion look like a football, with Americans divided but clustered around the middle? Or has it come to look like a dumbbell, with more people at the extremes and fewer in the center?" He cites sociologists Paul DiMaggio, John Evans, and Bethany Bryson, who answer that question based on twenty years' worth of data from two periodic surveys of public opinion. "They found no change in the 'bimodality' of public opinion over the two decades. The football was not becoming a dumbbell."[7]

The Transpartisan Majority: A Different America
If voters are not as conflicted as their leaders, how large is the potential transpartisan political constituency?

The transpartisan constituency begins with thirty-nine percent of registered independents. We should add to this group most of the thirty-four percent of Americans over eighteen who have not registered to vote. These figures total fifty-eight million independents and seventy-three million unregistereds, equaling 131 million people disassociated from the major parties in a country where 125 million voted for president in 2004.[8]

This majority of constitutionally eligible voters not affiliated with the major parties is broadened by the thousands of Republican and Democratic Party members who are as disgusted by ugly partisanship as are the citizen critics who turn away from party affiliations and even from politics itself.

The data reviews by Rauch and Fiorina make it clear that Americans occupy a political world larger and more diverse than that allowed by the two-party system entrusted with representing them. Neither partisan attitudes nor partisan voting accurately speaks for this powerful transpartisan impulse at a time of profound political transformation. Our political institutions and the media, armed with agendas that artificially encourage, magnify and highlight conflict, systematically conceal agreement and discourage cooperation across current ideologically-proclaimed party lines. Although there are powerful indications of a desire to cooperate, political leaders systematically ignore, and even suppress, attempts to promote cooperation.

Faced with great voter dissatisfaction and with a large, untapped political constituency waiting to be discovered, why have more collaborative political leaders not appeared to appeal to them? Why are our political leaders (with some conspicuous exceptions) so doggedly wedded to conflict?

One of the most important reasons is that conflict produces rewards. While many political partisans believe they are serving the public interest, others have substantial, vested interests in conflict. Their interest comes from dividing spoils created by a system that focuses all attention on government and the favors it can dispense. Even, or perhaps especially, when an issue is principled, the partisans administering closely-divided governments make every issue a cliffhanger and every action wrenching. Thus, partisan bickering, wheeling, dealing, and playing to partisan crowds often ends in great personal gain for its practitioners, while often (if not usually) ignoring the values of real Americans and their desire to share responsibility for solving problems in public spaces.

Morris Fiorina reaches similar conclusions. Politics is out of touch with Americans, Fiorina says, because it "usually reflects an unrepresentative political class of...officeholders, interest-group leaders, political info-tainers, and issue activists – people in these roles constitute a political class that often represents the public face of politics in America." This is the fiercely partisan political power elite that is profoundly out of touch with the American people.

Language: Partly a Problem of Words

The problem, we believe, begins with language. We believe that the American political vocabulary and its governing concepts – "conservative right" and "liberal left" – have neither conceptual clarity nor practical relevance since each concept contains contradictory meanings, and neither represents real people, individually or collectively.

We suggest replacing the simple left-right spectrum with the matrix described by A. Lawrence Chickering, co-author of this essay, in his 1993 book *Beyond Left and Right.*[9] Chickering argued that not two but four positions – a "freedom" position and an "order" position on both the left and the right – compete for political allegiance in our system.

The freedom right tends to focus on reason – the order right on tradition and faith. The freedom right are the free market, libertarian conservatives, who embrace the modernist values of individualism, freedom, reason, progress and rights. Examples would begin with the late economist Milton Friedman and, in fact, with economists as a group. The order right are traditional, often religious, conservatives – and on many issues neoconservatives – who believe that modern problems result from the assault on traditional virtues by the very modernist values embraced by "conservatives" on the freedom right. They would include religious leaders like the late Jerry Falwell (the Moral Majority) and many neoconservatives (Irving Kristol, Seymour Martin Lipset, and many others).

A similar conflict may be found on the left between the order (or social democratic) left and the freedom (or civil libertarian) left. The freedom left includes both advocacy groups for individual rights such as the American Civil Liberties Union (ACLU) and anti-government counter-culturists, some of whom identify themselves as "left-libertarians." Both of these freedom left groups are radical decentralizers suspicious of large organizations, both public and private, and opposing the mechanistic, material ambitions of the order left as well as those of the order right. The order left, for example, leans toward national plans such as requirements to buy health insurance while the free left is more inclined to a national health plan that allows choice.

Rauch reached a similar conclusion about conflict, both between the parties and within them. He also notes that the struggle about values is going on within individuals. He writes:

By no means, then does partisan parity necessarily imply a deeply divided citizenry. People who talk about culture wars usually have in mind not merely a close division (50/50) but a wide or deep division – two populations with distinct and incompatible world views. ...One 'orthodox,' the other 'progressive'. ... One faction emphasizes duty and morality; another stresses individual rights and self-fulfillment...the result is a 'values divide' – indeed, a 'chasm'. ... [He quotes sociologist Alan Wolfe as saying] 'The two sides presumed to be fighting the culture war do not so much represent a divide between one group of Americans and another as a divide between sets of values important to everyone.'

These conflicts within both left and right explain why "conservatives" and "liberals" can be found on all sides of almost every major issue, as both the Fiorina and Rauch data indicate. "Conservatives" can be found both passionately for and passionately against the Iraq War, gay marriage, increasing international trade, and countless other issues. Libertarians like the late Milton Friedman and the Cato Institute opposed the war from the beginning.[10] Part of the order right, including neoconservatives, have generally supported the war, while an isolationist strain leads traditional conservatives like Pat Buchanan to oppose the war. The freedom right likes the fact that markets operating efficiently tend to be "value neutral," while the order right often sees markets eroding traditional values.

"Liberals" can also be found voting for and against the resolution authorizing the Iraq war,[11] gay marriage,[12] globalization,[13] and countless other issues.

These conflicts within both the left and right cause theoretical as well as practical difficulties for both. The theoretical problems are obvious. They arise when it becomes difficult to say what a "conservative" or "liberal" believes. But beyond theory and language, large practical problems arise for both when they try to govern.

The most obvious tension disturbing the current, "conservative" administration relates to its prosecution of the war in Iraq. It is a project most supported by the order right, a project which has greatly increased the size and power of government. Still, following the freedom right, the administration continues to encourage people to distrust the government, a stance that weakens its authority in prosecuting its war policy. The president does this almost every time he advocates lower taxes and reduced spending.

The greatest practical problem facing Democrats and the left when they are in power arises when the order left tries to sell government as the instrument for promoting social justice against the freedom left's unrelenting commitment, like libertarians of the freedom right, to encourage people to distrust the government. Anti-government agitation by the freedom wings of both the left and right thus complicates important priorities in the policy agendas of the order wings of both.

A classic example of conflict between order and freedom impulses on the left occurred when the Clinton Administration embraced welfare reform. *The Washington Post* called this initiative a dramatic "devolution" of responsibility – turning what used to be a federal, centralized system over to the states. Clinton himself, on its tenth anniversary, hailed his welfare reform as a bipartisan achievement that shrank welfare rolls and put single mothers to work. Nevertheless, many liberals attacked the new law as draconian, and several key "liberal" Clinton supporters quit high-level government posts in protest.

When one side or the other is in power, strong incentives exist for their freedom and order wings to paper over their differences and even deny them. That describes how George W. Bush, directed by his political advisor Karl Rove, has, until recently, been able to hold in lock-step – under one "conservative" banner – such diverse, often contradictory, beliefs. But when the contradictions start to weaken the coherence of the party's program – as is happening now to the Republicans and (to pick a striking example from the past) as happened to the Democrats at the end of the 1960s – the contradictions tend to erupt into open conflict.

What forces drive the conflict between freedom and order? Chickering argued that the conflict serves both left and right in their search for integration of the two sets of values that are centrally important to both all modern societies and to all modern people.

The integration of rights and responsibilities – or freedom and order – presents the great challenge to, and opportunity for, the emergence of a new transpartisan politics.

CHAPTER TWO

SOME CASUALTIES OF PARTISAN POLITICS:
PRISONS, SCHOOLS, HOSPITALS, & NATIONAL SECURITY

We begin our discussion of transpartisan opportunities with four examples of partisan failure: prisons, schools, hospitals, and national security. The pattern of failure in these examples may be found across much of the spectrum of political issues and problems. We have drawn these examples from real experiences. These stories highlight problems but also suggest possibilities for change.

Prisons and the Penal System

The debate on penal reform has followed a familiar pattern, largely unchanged, for half a century if not much longer. The broad architecture of the debate pits one side, "conservatives" and their institutions, (police departments and sheriffs' offices), emphasizing personal responsibility for crime and advocating more punishment and more prison, against "liberals" or "progressives," emphasizing the value of rehabilitation and advocating economic and social reforms to get at the "underlying causes" of crime. The debate and the conflicting arguments are so familiar that everybody can lip-sync them.

Though the debate has gone on for decades, with little sense of movement or fresh insight, the facts about crime are alarming. The United States Crime Index Rates (per 100,000 inhabitants) went from 1,887.2 in 1960 to 5,897.8 in 1991. In 1960 these rates were 1.89 percent of being a victim of a crime and 0.161 percent of becoming victim of a violent crime. By 1991 the crime rate was 313 percent of the 1960 crime rate. In 1996 your risk of being a victim of a crime in the United States was 5.079 percent, and of a violent crime 0.634 percent.[1]

Our crime rate is higher than that of any other advanced nation. Among the leading industrialized nations our murder rate is three and one half times higher than the second place nation, Italy. The USA has a higher percentage of its citizens behind bars than any other nation. The majority of persons released from prison in the U.S. (estimates run as high as seventy percent) are convicted of new crimes within five years.[2] Neither the ongoing debate nor the reality has changed, and everybody knows it. As a result, the issues of crime and penal reform have all but disappeared from our active political debate.

In Santa Barbara, California, a group of reformers, led by retired businessman Rick Roney, decided to try a very different approach in mid-2005.

"We started by doing a statewide Field Poll that showed the public was open to change." Roney recalled. "The public had figured out that the current system was broken. They thought that inmates leaving prison were more likely to commit a crime than before they went into prison. They also felt the best (and lowest long term cost) prison policy was punishment combined with in-prison and post-prison rehabilitation. They favored this by an eight-to-one margin. We took those results to Sacramento. In Sacramento," Roney recalled, "we wanted to explore some new approaches. Rod Hickman, at the time Secretary of California Department of Corrections and Rehabilitation (CDCR), was an enthusiastic reformer, but changing the bureaucracy was very difficult. As Hickman said, 'We're hard to help!'"

After six months, they gave up and returned to Santa Barbara County to focus on the issue of prisoners reentering into the community after they leave prison. "Reentry is essentially a local issue," Roney said. "There is nothing Sacramento or CDCR can do to get a parolee a place to live, a job, or enrollment in a substance abuse treatment program. And the price paid when new crimes are committed by parolees is paid by the local community – crime costs, victims, law enforcement, courts."

Since they could see how truly local the issue is, and since they could see that bureaucratic resistance to change made it clear the government would provide no leadership on the issue, they returned to Santa Barbara County. "Back home," Roney said, "we found some powerful ways to motivate a variety of interest groups to want to do something." They went to essentially all the stakeholders in the county – sheriff, police, parole, probation, district attorney, community-based service providers, community colleges, and businesses. They would say: "Santa Barbara County has 750-1000 inmates returning from state prison every year to Santa Barbara County. Seventy percent of them will be back in prison within three years. Is that a problem? Do you want to help develop a solution?" Every single person said "yes" to both questions.

When they started, there was little interest in the issue as a local issue. "People regarded crime and especially the penal system as *state issues*," Roney said. To counter the lack of interest, they started by gathering information that would go beyond the superficialities and abstractions of the current debate and might encourage people to see *their* stake in the issue.

The most important information they found was the statistic that ninety-eight percent of prison inmates, when they are released, return to their local community; three-quarters of them then return to crime and to prison. "This provided the ammunition to bring together a working group of civic leaders representing different groups concerned about crime," Roney said. "The statistic that ninety-eight percent of criminals return to their homes made it clear to everyone that the state government had neither any interest nor capacity to work effectively to reintegrate these former prison inmates into society. Because three-quarters of them will continue committing crimes, we in Santa Barbara had both the interest and the capacity to do something." Roney continued:

> We now have a functioning Santa Barbara County Reentry Project. The sheriff, DA, three Police departments, Parole, Probation, a nationally acclaimed reentry expert and two community providers are on the Steering Committee. It's been funded — partially privately, partially with state CDCR funds. We contact inmates in prison six to nine months prior to their release and ask them if they want to change their lives and become functioning members of the community. We tell them we're willing to help if they do. If they sign up, we then develop a personalized re-entry plan for that inmate. What does he/she need upon release? Substance abuse treatment (eighty-five percent chose this), a job, a place to live (again eighty-five percent need this), family reconciliation, etc.
>
> A case manager arranges for these things to be available upon the inmates release. (One big problem is normally a parolee returning into the community who signs up for a substance abuse treatment program or clean/sober living arrangement has to wait three to four weeks before admittance. By then it's too late!) The case manager meets with the project participant weekly for one year to help him/her be successful meeting his/her goals. We have been receiving inmates since April 2007 and have about sixty in the program. We're measuring results. We have a control group. So in two to three years we'll know if we're making a difference.

Although the story is still unfolding, it is interesting for several reasons. First, people who avoided all contact with one another, and mostly called each other names, started actively working together to develop a solution upon which they could all agree. And these people, who in the public mainstream debate were supposedly locked in relentless conflict, actually came to a common understanding of what is wrong and what to do about it.

"At the outset," Roney noted, "these very different groups were able to agree by focusing on the easiest cases and by avoiding the more difficult ones." They organized a program that would track every returning inmate. Their common understanding was that *isolation* and *disconnection* were critical causes of alienation and crime. They concluded that the best antidotes to these problems lay in creation of support systems for returning inmates.

The politics of this commitment are especially interesting. The "conservatives" who emphasized punishment in the general, abstract debate joined the "liberals" in reaching out to the returning inmates, because both groups were motivated by a desire to reduce the crime committed by returning inmates.

This common commitment at the outset was limited to the easiest cases. Those convicted of the violent crimes and sex offenders were excluded from the system. But these returning inmates posed the greatest threat to the community. So, before long, a representative of the sheriff's office asked why the violent offenders should be excluded. He emphasized that since they were the greatest threat, the group should be *most* concerned to help them, "and we were only helping those that wanted to change and asked for help, not deciding whether they should be released or not." Roney reported one member of the Steering Committee, a long time advocate of reentry and rehabilitation, said she had never, in thirty years, heard a law enforcement official take a position in favor of rehabilitation.

In this process, the Santa Barbara group has found an important role for state officials, who have taken great interest in the experiment. As a result, the CDCR has given the group a grant of $625,000 over three years to pay for parolee services. Also, with the passage of Governor Schwarzenegger's Prison

Reform Legislation in June of 2007, the state is now committed to building "secure reentry facilities" in local communities around California. These facilities will house inmates during their last twelve months of incarceration. They will provide extensive services to inmates to prepare them for life after prison, such as life skills programs, job training, and substance abuse treatment. They are situated in communities so as to involve the local community in this process. This will work seamlessly with the Reentry Project. CDCR has made the Santa Barbara County Reentry Project a key part of their statewide education process about reentry facilities.[3]

This citizen-engaged Santa Barbara program succeeds because of an active concept of citizenship. It stands in sharp contrast to the abstract, state-centered position that dominates the issue of penal reform almost everywhere — one that both reflects and encourages a weak concept of citizenship. Which system has a better chance to socialize criminals into the society: 1) a system run by distant bureaucrats with no personal contacts with the returning inmates, or 2) a system that engages the local community and encourages it to accept responsibility for returning inmates? The answer is obvious.

Public Schools: A 'Rising Tide of Mediocrity'

Conservatives and liberals agree that our public schools are in crisis. Unfortunately, neither has the slightest idea what to be *"for"* in reforming the schools. Both know what they *oppose*, however. Conservatives favor creating alternative schools — either charter schools or through vouchers. Liberals oppose vouchers, and many liberals even oppose charter schools. Conservatives believe no reforms exist to make public schools workable; therefore public school policy should free families from having to send their children to failing institutions. Liberals argue that allowing children to leave is worse than forcing them to stay, especially for those left behind (the disadvantaged).

The current debate has degenerated into conservatives looking for ways out of the current system and liberals investing all their energy on opposing conservatives. Neither is effectively looking to discover workable solutions in current schools that are failing.

The 1983 U.S. Department of Education report, *A Nation at Risk*, stated the basic challenge as follows: "Our nation is at risk. Our once unchallenged preeminence in commerce, industry, science, and technological innovation is being overtaken by competitors throughout the world. ... The educational foundations of our society are presently being eroded by a rising tide of mediocrity that threatens our very future as a nation and a people."[4]

It has been more than twenty-five years since the publication of *A Nation at Risk*, with its clarion call for school reform. Yet little has happened since then because most reform proposals stimulate powerful opposition. The tragic state of our schools is underscored by the appalling statistic that one-half of all public school teachers leave teaching within five years! Many of them leave to take lower paying jobs teaching in private schools. Real reform needs to come from a completely new reform strategy. This new strategy for reform begins by understanding its opponents.

Conservatives and many liberals commonly say that the public school problem lies with either teachers' unions or the administrative bureaucracy overseeing the schools. This argument is predicated on the problem of centralized power: People with power (the analysis goes) want to hold on to it; so the system goes unreformed. As a result, the tide of mediocrity continues to rise. The recommendations of *A Nation at Risk*, a report (according to its authors) "free of political partisanship ... flounder in a partisan sea."[5]

The notion that public bureaucrats and public school teachers are like monopoly capitalists who won't give up their power is absurd. If they are so privileged, why aren't they having more fun? Could it be that their power is illusory?

In reality, they live in a nightmare, mechanistic world – brittle, lifeless and pinched. Remember those public school teachers that leave teaching within five years? Many report finding it more gratifying to wait tables than to teach kids. The word "mechanistic" plays a central role in our critique of the partisan deadlock that characterizes subject after subject in the "conservative/liberal" policy formation arena. By "mechanistic" we mean machine-like – minimizing the uniquely personal while promoting statistical norms as the currency of success and failure. We contrast it to "organic," "connected," and "vibrant." Machines are dead. Organic is alive. Machines are useful as tools. They fail as substitutes for life.

Understanding the challenge of reforming schools requires understanding this paradox: Many people inside the system who want change so much are in such pain that they cannot tolerate change. In this mechanistic nightmare, people are so unhappy that any prospect of sudden change overloads them, so most of them say no to any change. The public policy reform model, a mechanical model of convulsive change engineered by governments over which partisans fight, itself is the major culprit here. A different model of change is needed to reform the schools.

Our communities know how to run successful public schools, even in severely economically disadvantaged neighborhoods. The challenge is to transfer the models of success into operating public schools. What model of change can work?

One model that is working in many individual public schools and in hundreds of government schools in India is a grass-roots, incremental model – a model in which change happens organically and consensually by action of all major stakeholders at individual schools.[6] In this model, teachers, parents, administrators and children work together to improve the school. This model is being used in many public schools today, and, in our experience, because all major parties to the change are included, it is almost never opposed.

James Dierke, principal of Visitacion Valley Middle School in San Francisco, exemplifies this approach in his leadership of a school that is in the most dangerous neighborhood in the city (forty-one murders last year). He became principal in 2000 and faced a demoralized community with rock-bottom test scores, teachers leaving, and every other indication of a dysfunctional inner-city school. An excellent symbol of the problems at Visitacion Valley was that when he arrived at this school, there were sixteen students taking algebra, and all of them were Asian girls (this in an enrollment that was fifty percent black). Today, everyone in the school takes algebra, morale is high, and in 2008 Dierke won an award as the outstanding principal of a middle school in all of the United States. How did he do it? He honored his people, brought them into the decision-making process, and gave them responsibility. He moved slowly, but steadily (the axiom of organic change). He insisted that all of his kids could learn, and told them that he would "not give up" on anyone.

Opening spaces for real self-governance, including real responsibility for parents, teachers and administrators at individual schools, offers a powerful reform model that has been demonstrated to work in many schools, not just at Visitacion Valley. Because it empowers teachers at the school, teachers' unions support it. And because it works one by one, school by school, it tends to draw little resistance from centralized education bureaucracies.

A key to this model of change is the empowerment of parents to play an active role in schools. This empowerment model tends to succeed when it extends to parents both rights and responsibilities.

Obstacles to importing these lessons may be found at different levels: 1) in the cultures of individual schools, which are afraid of change; 2) in bureaucratic opposition to permitting schools more authority over their own programs at school system administrative levels; and 3) in state bureaucratic opposition to allowing flexibility, to name a few. We do not want to pretend that there are no impediments to this reform model, but if implemented in a way that follows the experiences of schools that have had success using it, this model can make powerful contributions to the reform process within individual schools. Enlightened leadership at the local, district and state levels can also play an important role in promoting this kind of reform.

While many public school activists oppose charter schools, most public school teachers would like to have the authority and responsibilities that teachers in most charter schools commonly enjoy. In the current system, public school teachers are often forced to behave like robots, acting out the decisions made by distant bureaucracies, often influenced by the lobbying of textbook publishers, as partisans fight over state and federal education dollars. All of this dysfunction is destroying the education of our children. *No Child Left Behind*, the current federal education program, broadens and deepens the mechanistic gulf in American education by, as James Dierke puts it, *failing to address the whole child.*

The Healthcare System

The July 26, 2000, issue of *The Journal of the American Medical Association* (JAMA), featured a paper by Dr. Barbara Starfield, senior professor of medicine at Johns Hopkins School of Hygiene and Public Health, which argued that medical errors may be the third leading cause of death in the United States.[7] The principal errors included more than 100,000 deaths per year from adverse effects of drugs and 80,000 deaths per year from infections in hospitals.

The U.S. medical system, sometimes referred to as a "health care system," fails in the same way our education system fails. In its "mechanistic" structure, it is less concerned with promoting health than with fighting disease. This is a crucial point in understanding what is wrong with the U.S. medical system. Whatever the desires are of the people who work within, the system itself has almost no interest in promoting health, and both its resources and the surrounding system of incentives are all focused on fighting disease through the performance of expensive operations and the prescription of expensive drugs.

Brian Salmon, a Perfusion Assistant from Chicago, reports that he came down with cancer, got some help with the costs from his health insurance, though it still took him years to pay off the thousands of dollars of out-of-pocket costs. After three years of follow-up visits, his insurance company said they no longer considered his hospital, where he had developed a relationship with the doctors, nurses, and staff, a provider for their plans. People who had been there during some of the toughest times of his life were lost to him. The mechanistic triumphed.[8]

Evonne Hilton, from Seattle, says, "I'm frustrated by the healthcare system." Five years ago, Hilton fell and severely injured her head. She was in a managed healthcare system. The doctors didn't do a diagnostic scan; she was seen in the emergency room and was discharged without further treatment. She found herself unable to do her job due to severe memory loss and inability to function. She tried for several years to do other jobs within the organization but finally had to quit. "I lost everything. No one would hire me. I was on the street for years." Medicaid kicked in last year. She now lives on social security disability in a Seattle Housing Authority apartment. She is able to pick her doctor and hospital. She suffers chronic daily headaches, a sometimes severe and disabling condition which affects about one in six people in the U.S.[9]

Since the system focuses all of its energy on cost-maximizing surgeries, procedures and drugs, it is not surprising that the U.S. medical system is the most expensive in the world — almost twice as expensive as Switzerland, the second most expensive. At the same time, it ranks thirty-fifth in the world by international standards, twenty-fourth in life expectancy and twenty-sixth in infant mortality. Not only is it the most expensive medical system, it is the least (or second to the least, depending on the specific measure) effective system among industrial nations in promoting health.[10]

The problem in medicine is precisely the same as in education and prisons. And so is the solution. The key in school reform is to empower teachers, parents, administrators, and children at individual schools in local communities. Local communities organized to support stakeholders are also key to reforming the medical system so that it promotes *health* by encouraging people to take responsibility for their own health. How important is personal responsibility to health? Here is what Professor Walter M. Bortz II, says about this: "The older you become, the more you realize how unimportant the doctor is in the whole business of growing older. Your ancestors contribute twenty percent to the extent of your life, your physician provides another ten to twenty percent, and you determine the rest. Living longer is a choice, not fate."[11] If we remove genetic factors (which you cannot influence) from Dr. Bortz's calculations, medical care accounts for twelve to twenty-four percent of health, and how people take care of themselves accounts for the rest!

Just as centralized, educational bureaucracies have created a centralized, mechanical nightmare in education, and centralized prisons have created the same for crime and justice, the U.S. health bureaucracy is creating a similar centralized, mechanical, and expensive nightmare in health care. Entrenched partisans thrive on the battle over healthcare dollars just as they do over education and prison dollars. As a result, we lack optimal education, optimal crime prevention, and optimal health. Reforming the U.S. health care system offers additional opportunities for transpartisan initiatives.

The figures below help explain why we overspend on medicine, as we do on schools and prisons and yet we have so comparatively little social value to show for it. In 1998 The

U.S. health system spent $4,178 for each patient it treated. Switzerland, spent $2,794. The Organization for Economic Cooperation and Development median was $1,783. Despite its lead in cost per patient, U.S. health lags behind virtually all industrial countries in the quality of the health of its people. In a shocking study that underscored the failure of the American health care system entitled "Why Americans Die," Professor C. David Jenkins of the University of North Carolina, concluded from international health statistics that in every decade of life – one to ten, eleven to twenty, twenty-one to thirty, etc. – Americans die more frequently than do the people in dozens of other nations. The reasons for these health care failures track directly the failures of the education and prison systems.

In trying to understand these statistics, one might look at the standard of health used by the World Health Organization (WHO), of which the U.S. is a member. WHO has a very good sense about the real, contributing factors to health. It believes that health is a state of positive physical, mental and social well-being, not merely the absence of disease or infirmity. The U.S. health care system has not yet integrated this definition into its medical theory and practice, and its failure to move beyond its war against disease model explains much of the reason why it fails.

Science increasingly is discovering the unique organic characteristics of each individual's health as well as the specific treatment intervention and healthy lifestyle each person needs. The formal name for this is "biochemical individuality." Nevertheless, the mechanistic health care system continues treating diseases and behaving as if people have little or no role to play in their own health. It fails to treat the whole person and instead insists on mechanistically treating symptoms while ignoring how to work with patients and encourage them to lead healthy lives. This approach echoes Socrates' criticism of doctors in the Athens of his time for their failure to treat the "whole man."

Although most of this discussion has been focused on doctors and hospitals, the insurance industry has an enormous role to play in encouraging people to take care of themselves. When was the last time you were asked about diet and exercise when you applied for medical insurance?

Trust, connection, individual engagement and responsibility, essential components to effective education, and the response of communities to crime, need to be an intrinsic part of the healthcare system, as well. Tens of millions of Americans are seeking health and wellness support outside the standard medical model because they feel they are treated more honestly, completely, and with a connection to their health practitioner. Many of the practitioners these millions of Americans rely on are themselves leaving the standard medical system, often for less income. Fewer than thirty percent perhaps only twelve percent of American medical doctors currently belong to the American Medical Association.

National government policy might make an effective shift in health policy if, drawing on integrated, transpartisan values, it helped to promote lower cost, and more-connected health modalities. A couple of examples illustrate this opportunity.

Back pain is one of the most persistent problems affecting the industrial work force. The standard operation undertaken to correct back pain costs about $30,000. Treatment for back pain by acupuncture costs about $3,000. In one small study industrial workers complaining of back pain were offered the acupuncture treatment prior to getting surgery. Over two-thirds of those who chose acupuncture did not ultimately choose back surgery.

Dietary supplements can also provide cost-effective health improvements. For example, according to one estimate, one dollar's worth of vitamin A supplementation in third world countries provides social improvement equal to thirty dollars worth of developmental aid.

Health care is a very ripe area for the integrated, transpartisan values of freedom and responsibility. There is no reason we cannot become a healthier nation while spending less on health care if we reach beyond the confines of our current health care system and recruit citizens as active partners in promoting their own health. The current health system is failing for the same reason our public schools and our prison system are failing. The system is entirely mechanistic. It offers no effective opportunity or incentives for people to play an active role.

National Security

While we were writing this essay, the debate on national security and foreign policy showed signs that it might be shifting, at least on the central subject of Iraq. When we started, the debate was following the same pattern as the debates on prisons, education, and health care. It was all about governments and the international organizations that serve governments.

In Iraq all effort was focused on trying to get Iraq's weak government to effect a national reconciliation among the country's conflicted ethnic and religious groups: Sunnis, Shia, and Kurds. There was little or no place for local action on the part of citizens and civil society organizations (CSOs), where citizens might address economic, political and social problems in ways that could have international significance.

At the end of August 2007, reports started coming from Iraq that after four years of asking the weak central government to do things it could not or would not do (we think perhaps both), the U.S. Government was starting to see the importance of local action in promoting both opposition to Al Qaeda insurgents and possibly national reconciliation. We do not want to go too far with this point because it is still unclear whether the arming of now-friendly Sunnis in Anbar Province will create lasting instruments of peace and reconciliation, or activists in a civil war. (The answer may well depend on whether the central government allows separate groups the independence and self-governance that they want.)

The need to expand the vision of foreign policy beyond governments and states became especially obvious after 9/11, when it became clear that most of the new threats to U.S. and international security are now arising in countries with weak or illegitimate governments yet strong societies. These weak states present very different challenges from those of the strong states that were our adversaries in the past.*

While the foreign policy traditionally implemented among strong states has worked in the past, it does not work between a strong state and a weak state. Strong states don't have the experience or on-the-ground resources to quickly and successfully interact with the strong societies of weak states. Strong states don't have the knowledge or up-to-date information on who are the major influencers and power brokers both within the strong societies and within government. How can strong states understand the complex relationships among a variety of disparate groups which somehow enable the countries to function? How can effective relationships be built between members of strong states and the strong societies of weak states so that trust and a resultant policy shift can occur?

Often, out of frustration, strong states use force to try and get their way (as in Iraq and Lebanon) because they are unable to find answers to the questions we raised above, but the use of force actually weakens and divides the strong states while strengthening and coalescing the ones who are attacked. Is it any wonder that force often provokes a staunch resistance, particularly if it occurs in one's homeland? In the terribly destructive fighting in Lebanon, Hezbollah lost every battle, yet emerged stronger among the citizenry there. Similarly, the current U.S. posture toward Syria and Iran has effectively increased Arab and Muslim support for these countries, not isolated them.

----

* *"Failed states" are an extreme version of "weak states". Failed states like Somalia and Sudan are those in which there is very little central government authority, and formal institutions are largely broken.*

Of all the countries in the world, the United States, with its Minutemen, "Swamp Fox," "Green Mountain Boys," heritage, should understand the strategy and psychology that strong cultures within weak states can use to defeat the objectives of the strong states. In the United States' fervent crusade to democratize the world and create other strong nation-states, we forget the lesson to be learned from the birthing process of our own country: Strong societies can — and most often will — dominate weak nation-states, and can give even strong states a run for their money.

In dealing with weak states, foreign policy makers must expand their intellectual horizons and attempt to influence societies and cultures as well as states. This means formulating two separate policies, one for states and one for societies. Conventional foreign policy should address the *objective* interests of states, and the other address the largely *subjective* challenges of societies and cultures.

Failure to address the separate, often largely subjective, challenges of societies explains the enormous fatalism that marks the current debate on foreign policy. At a time when technology, media and economic progress are empowering non-state actors, empowering the "street," and amplifying the power of public opinion, failure to engage non-state actors and societies leaves government policymakers with unhappy and highly limited alternatives. On one side are the administration's "tough" policies: avoiding or greatly limiting contact with both unfriendly regimes (Palestine, Syria, Iran) and significant non-state actors (Hezbollah, Muslim Brotherhood in Egypt, various groups in Iraq) that are in conflict with friendly regimes. On the other side is the Democrats' and some Republicans' "soft" eagerness to negotiate with unfriendly regimes (Syria, Iran) without understanding their constraints as weak states.

A 2006 study of civil society and foreign policy outlined a strategy for working with civil society organizations to promote economic, social and political reform in developing countries.[12] Some of the initiatives aim at promoting certain kinds of government policies (economic policy reform and property rights for the poor), while others aim at promoting changes in society and culture (educating girls and programs to recruit citizens in promoting democracy and peace). These programs suggest the beginning seeds of transpartisan policy initiatives that can engage the American transpartisan majority and empower the "Transpartisan Imperative" in both domestic and national security policy.

Perhaps the most heralded civil society initiative promoting economic, social and political change in developing countries is the program developed by Peruvian Hernando de Soto and his Instituto Libertad y Democracia (ILD) to promote property rights for the poor. Although it is described in two international best-selling books – and financed largely by USAID – U.S. foreign policy has almost completely ignored de Soto's program, which is committed to objectives identical with U.S. foreign policy objectives, and which also enjoys almost universal support by the governments and non-state sectors of developing countries.[13]

The overall purpose of these activities should be to promote social trust and reduce internal conflict, expand loyalty and identity beyond family and tribe, and thus promote development of a culture conducive to both economic and political development.

Carrying out these recommendations will be enormously demanding for foreign policymakers and for the foreign policy community generally. The government institutions devoted to foreign affairs were designed for very different challenges. Today, problems in what the Pentagon is calling "the Long War" come primarily from a multitude of unknown, often invisible, non-state actors (ethnic, religious, terrorist, criminal and patriotic) as well as from weak states. The impulse of conservatives and liberals alike is to debate about ways to act that would be appropriate for dealing with strong state adversaries. When taken against weak states, these actions can produce large, unintended consequences, weakening our security or causing us to miss opportunities to strengthen it.

The Iraq Study Group proposed negotiations with Iran and Syria in an effort to enlist their support in reducing conflict in Iraq. The Bush administration has remained committed to a confrontational approach to those countries. Both positions, the more "liberal" Iraq Study Group approach and the more "conservative" Bush administration approach, overstate the power of these weak states and fail to lay the groundwork for formal negotiations through informal contacts with civil society. Strong contacts and engagement with civil society would expand the possibilities for positive outcomes of formal negotiations and would limit the risks associated with them.

Developing policies for societies means working with civil society organizations to promote reform of government policies, and to change social and cultural attitudes. Ultimately, however, these initiatives must be directed toward influencing states as well, because even when the objective is to change society and culture, active government cooperation is essential to accomplishing anything at strategic scales.

At present, civil society organizations* (CSOs) and policies toward societies and cultures have little if any significant role in the larger debate on international relations and foreign policy.[14] Part of the reason is a lack of understanding about the strategic significance of civil society and a limited understanding of what is possible. The foreign policy community takes a fatalistic view of cultures, assuming there is little or nothing it can do to affect them, and limits its analyses to observation without any pre-

---

* *CSOs are involved in legal reform initiatives, legal aid, environmental research and advocacy, moderate Islamic associations, business and labor associations, public health, educational associations, conflict resolution, sports, community organizations, religious groups, and so forth.*

scription for corrective action. Raising the banner of culture, for most people, means there is little you can do but wait and hope.

These are classic Burkean conservative warnings, now ironically expressed by liberals when critiquing the Bush administration's ambitious plans to promote democracy in the developing world. Yet the warnings are overdrawn. Our proposals are based on a considerable body of knowledge about, and experience with, models of civil society action in many countries that have demonstrated feasibility, potential scale, and costs consistent with powerful strategic impacts.

Bringing Citizens into Public Spaces

The day of public policy restricted to government action has passed. As Hernando de Soto has remarked, "Democracy has got to be about more than just electing dictators every four years." While it is obvious that some areas of policy need to be for governments alone – fighting wars, controlling the money supply, enacting a tax code – in many areas, citizens must become an active part of serious efforts to solve economic, political and social problems. This imperative is important for several reasons: 1) because solutions without active citizen involvement are impossible to achieve or even imagine; 2) because engaged citizen participation will reduce conflict in our politics; 3) because active citizen involvement in public life is part of a healthy, modern democracy; and finally, 4) because citizens are demanding it.

The mechanistic institutions run only by governments deaden political and social life, demoralize everyone forced to be dead, and inflame conflict from people in acute pain from life without real, human contact.

The chapters in Part II examine major issues, explain why we are failing, and suggest what it will take to succeed. The chapters provide a taste of the more detailed discussion of the transpartisan imperative set out in Parts IV and V.

Part II

The Old Politics: Squeezing the Life Out of Society

In the next three chapters we focus on major issue areas, highlighting problems that arise out of the terms of discussion. The most important of these is the tendency in our political debate to regard "public" and "government" as meaning the same thing. Focusing exclusively on the government and excluding citizens is what produces the mechanistic political system that alienates everyone, including those who work for the government.

Part III puts these issues in historical and philosophical context, and Part IV looks beyond problems to solutions and explores how transpartisan approaches, engaging citizens as partners with governments, can begin to solve problems that now seem unsolvable.

CHAPTER THREE

TRANSPARTISAN CAPITALISM I

For nearly two centuries political debate in the U.S. and other Western countries has been about "state" versus "market": between activities that are thought to be the province of government (state) and those thought to be activities of the private sector (market). This conflict, which some people think about in terms of "capitalism" (markets) and "socialism" (state), is also associated with the private sector versus the public sector.

We tend to assume that relatively bright lines separate "public" (state) from "private" (market) activities. In the transpartisan vision, and in many analytical frameworks, these terms are abstract and have little philosophical or operational significance. In reality, they mean no more than the words "conservative" and "liberal" mean.

In fact, a second great debate within Western countries — the debate between labor and capital — transforms the state versus government continuum of behavior into a matrix. Cross the state/market horizontal axis with a vertical capital/labor axis and a matrix revealing four sets of actors appears. The Western economic debate contains actors of various shades of state supported capital and labor and free market capital and labor.

Consider "capitalism." Many people think it is simple: the "free market," private business. However, the free market and private business are not only not the same thing; they are often in absolute conflict. The freedom right constantly comments on the tension between business and the market because business often tries to manipulate the market, especially by seeking government intervention in it. One needs to be cautious about generalizing, but big business, simply because of its political power, probably acts more often against markets than does small business, which lacks the power.

The market is an institution of freedom (assuming, of course, that it is not controlled). Business is an institution of order. This chapter is about markets, not about business.

The same relationships also exist for states. States are supposed to be "public"; yet everyone knows that they are heavily influenced by private interests, and many government officials are much more animated by private interest than by public spirit.

Elements of "private" are often crucial to accomplish "public" purposes. While in some sectors we want government monopolies (the custodians of force, our military and police, are obvious examples), private citizens still have important roles to play. In other sectors (public education is perhaps the best example), a powerful, active role exists for citizens. However, here the separation of public and private in the public debate inhibits citizens from playing an active role, which is so important for schools to be successful.

In a transpartisan conception, "public" purposes depend essentially and profoundly on "private" connections and experiences. "Public" experiences like mixed-race, mixed-class friendships, and love (or, indeed, racial integration generally) do not happen impersonally and mechanically as a result of assertions of legal right. Such friendships and integration — when genuine and not just expedient — result from deeply personal organic connections and engagements. If one accepts this point, it is easy to understand why governments alone — relying on commands and appeals to legal right — have such a poor record of overcoming many of the most important public challenges we face. It is not that these objectives are so difficult to achieve; they are not. There can be achievement when governments encourage the engagement of people in private relationships and organize their institutions to be inclusive of those relationships.

The rigid separation of public and private, all too often, has caused the development of public institutions dominated by regulations and rules and featuring 1) impersonal, dead, "mechanical" cultures; 2) disempowered, depressed people; and 3) no meaningful integration. Public schools are the most tragic example of this separation. In the schools, all organized interest groups (bureaucrats and teachers' unions, especially) pursue their own, selfish interests, with little thought for the "good" of those institutions. The behavior of these organized interest groups, however, is widely misunderstood. It is widely believed they are concerned only with power. It is believed that they have power, and they won't share it. The real reason for their behavior, however, is very different. People in bureaucratic cultures are actually in pain because they are forced to behave as if they were dead. They long for change but can't tolerate it. They long for the very connection that everyone experiences in personal relationships.

Where can one find really "public" schools, as opposed to schools acting "publicly"? Where can one find school cultures suffused with public spirit and cultures that encourage mixed relationships forged by institutionalized communication across loyalties? One finds it everywhere in "private," inner-city, parochial schools with high rates of minority enrollments. One also finds it in government schools in traditional parts of rural India, where parents, teachers, and children all have "ownership" of their schools and work together to make them work for their kids. An extraordinary controlled experiment has just begun in Washington, DC, which may test these principles. The experiment is occurring because the Catholic Archdiocese of Washington, which is unable to continue financing all of its twenty-eight inner-city parochial schools, has proposed turning eight of them into charter schools as part of Washington's public unified school district. The whole of Washington's political class — conservatives and liberals, Democrats and Republicans — is supporting the experiment and hopes it will succeed. The question will be whether, over time, Washington's public school system will be able to avoid imposing the bureaucratic system that is killing public schools everywhere.

The key, ironically, will be to sustain those qualities of "public" within these schools that were strong when the Church owned them. There are reasons for thinking they may be able to retain much of the traditional culture by becoming quasi-charter schools in a city that is experimenting widely with charter schools. National education experts, according to *The Washington Post*, say, "The proposal could be a solution for other urban Catholic school systems around the country that have struggled with declining enrollment and rising operating costs." It could also be a remarkable opportunity for the entire nation to begin empowering the transpartisan educational agenda.

People in "public" institutions such as public schools depend on a "private," engaged culture to make them truly "public." People in the "private" sector depend on those same "public" relationships made truly human by private engagement. To succeed, both public and private schools need the same combination of public and private. It is hard to "objectify" something that needs to be "subjective." Personal engagements and meaningful connections are not always easy to describe in words, but they can be felt. And it is those feelings that must be somehow understood and communicated for progress to occur on any issue that depends on personal engagement.

It is interesting that the sectors most likely to become government monopolies work through "commands." They sustain powerful senses of community through "missions" which, for their success, depend on private, personal engagement (the military) or, that bring government authorities into close, engaged contact with the people they are helping (police). On the battlefield, soldiers' lives depend on their working in close cooperation with one another while suppressing individual, decision-making initiative. The sectors most amenable to public "monopolies," it would appear, tend to be those most closely connected to the control of violence.

In education, on the other hand, bureaucratic command structures not only disempower teachers from reaching out to individual students, but also stifle personal engagement. It is true not only within school communities, but within the educational bureaucracies themselves. Individual initiative, a characteristic generally associated with "private," is crucial if schools are to be successful throughout the system — both in the school communities and in the bureaucracies.

Both left and right buy into the rigid separation of "public" versus "private." The left buys in because it believes the public sector to be the sanctified domain of public spirit and wants to expand it, uncontaminated by private interest. The right buys in because it believes the private sector is the purest domain, and they seek, relentlessly, to expand it and to reduce the size of government.[1] These summaries of the left's support for government and the right's for the private sector are crude and subject to important qualifications and exceptions. In fact, the attitudes of both sides toward the "public" versus "private" sector debate depend on what *issue* is being debated. While conservatives don't like the role of government on many domestic issues (*e.g.*, social welfare programs), they strongly support the government on others, especially national defense. Their latter position is crucially obvious at the present time in their support for rapid increases in the defense budget to fight the war on terrorism — what the Pentagon is calling "the Long War." Their support is a major reason why the defense budget has increased more than forty percent under President George W. Bush.

Domestic spending, however, has also increased a great deal under this president. This president promoted domestic spending on a scale neither he nor the Republican majority in Congress would ever have tolerated if a Democrat had been president. Without judging whether they were necessary or wise policy choices, we think the large increases in domestic spending were *conservative* investments in public support for 'the Long War'. It is for good reason that the late, conservative sociologist Robert Nisbet observed that governments grow most in wartime.

Liberal attitudes toward government are also more complicated than commonly thought. Liberals strongly oppose government encroachment on civil liberties, mostly in the form of government surveillance of citizens, justified in the name of national security. This hostility to the government comes most powerfully from liberal Hollywood's movies portraying government officials as cutthroats and murderers.[2] But even on issues relating to social welfare and concern for the disadvantaged, liberals do not necessarily like *actual* governments; they like *mythical* governments that behave as if they were guided by the liberal imagination. Most liberals express dislike for actual governments – and often appear to hate them – especially government programs promoting social welfare. The only thing liberals seem to dislike even more than actual governments is the conservatives' efforts to limit government and restrict its efforts to help the disadvantaged.

These positions are not inconsistent. Liberals support government, often reluctantly, to negate conservative policies they think will abandon the disadvantaged. The truth is, both sides often take positions that abandon one group to save another – or in the *hope* of saving another. In short, each group appears to exist merely to mitigate the influence of the other.

Although there are many valuable arguments to be made between "state" and "market," they now conceal major truths on a variety of economic and social issues. This concealment both retards solutions to various problems and inhibits the emergence of agreements on many issues.

Private Interest and Public Good

The rigid separation of "public" and "private" conceals how *private interest can promote the public good*. We are not, here, focusing on Adam Smith's argument in *The Wealth of Nations* that the market's "hidden hand," working through private interest, benefits the whole of society. We agree with this, and we also agree with more recent arguments about using market mechanisms to achieve efficient outcomes even on environmental issues.[3] These arguments, however, are about private interest narrowly understood as benefiting only the "actor." We are interested in circumstances in which private interest and public spirit overlap. *This happens when private interest is itself served by public spirit.*

Adam Smith wrote about this, too – though not in *The Wealth of Nations*. He wrote about it twenty years earlier, in *The Theory of Moral Sentiments*, when he considered the role of *empathy* in moral systems. Empathy arises with *personal contact and engagement*. This quality tends to be weak in traditional cultures because, being traditional, they operate out of habit: they do what they do because that is what they have always done. Living by habit, they neither communicate outside nor across loyalties; so they are limited in their contact with, or concern for, what is "public."

When people start to communicate consciously, they start to experience empathy and social trust. And, as people expand their communication to "other loyalties," empathy and social trust expands.[4] This phenomenon is absent throughout traditional societies (some of which now pose a major challenge to our security). The essential point here is that public spirit is most powerfully promoted in *private experiences*. For example, promoting tolerance across racial and religious lines can be encouraged by personal engagement that stimulates empathy and *spiritual connections*. (People who don't like the word "spiritual" might substitute for it the word "human.")

The key ingredient in promoting such personal engagement is *ownership* — a real, authoritative stake in making public spaces truly public, with empowered people collaborating to make those spaces, such as schools, living, positive communities.

It is at this point that private interest and public spirit come together and become one.* Conscious, personal engagement and connection — which we are associating here with public spirit — is not only *aligned* with private interest, but at the very *heart* of purpose and meaning in modern life. It is what people live for. (The word "modern" is crucial in the last sentence, but the power of the point is made clear as people in traditional societies, when given a chance, commit themselves to the trust and connection that we associate with being "modern."[5])

Public spaces, like schools, run bureaucratically, can become mechanical cultures in which disempowered people often live a nightmare with little human contact. Their lives are not unlike the lives in traditional societies, where decisions are made by habit and through conscious obedience to rules, with

----

* *It is common for people to understand private interest and public spirit as opposite in their definitions, not capable of integration. However, these two concepts can be integrated in several ways, all of them important. First, every healthy person has a private, empathic interest in doing things for other people without hope of reciprocal gain: ordinary kindnesses are common examples, tipping in restaurants, and so on. Engaging and connecting with people, even with strangers, itself is an example of private interest integrating with public spirit. The most important opportunity for this integration, however, comes when institutions empower people with real authority to engage each other in the design and implementation of policies for the institution. This happens a lot in nongovernment organizations. Governments need to do much more of it, so that "public spaces" can become much more genuinely public.*

little communication across loyalties. A powerful vocabulary, appealing to "equity" and "justice," conceals the brutality of this world without human contact. It is a world in which people honor each other publicly and objectively, because the system forces them to through politically correct language and behaviors. But it is a world marked by internal segregation and private rejection. It is a world devoid of the connection and engagement that are essential when people really honor and value each other and when they achieve real equality as human beings, even as they may possess very different resources. This is objective, mechanical life, removed desperately far from the subjective connections and meanings that are rooted in what people value most.

The "disempowered people" in this world include all of the principal actors in education: parents, teachers, children, administrators, and even bureaucrats. They are compelled to express a "public spirit" that is fake, and this fake, nightmare world often becomes a world of narrow, private interest. If some readers are inclined to object and argue that the bureaucrats, surely, are empowered, we strongly disagree. They are disempowered because their only power is the power to say "no." They have neither the power to live with any real authority outside the tyranny of bureaucratic rules nor the power to reach out to people they "oversee" to help empower them to solve their own problems.

People want to control their own lives. They want to make a difference. Mechanical cultures disempower everyone in them. Fortunately, empowerment is not a zero-sum game; in fact, it is often the opposite. The empowerment of bureaucrats depends on their success in helping promote the empowerment of those they oversee, for their power comes not in giving commands, but in personal engagement.

Liberals tend to believe that public spirit results from generalized appeals and from government programs marketed as "for the public good." In reality, however, public spaces such as public schools are rife with narrow bureaucratic interest, high distrust, and little of the sense of real community that is essential to real public spirit. Conservatives believe public spirit occurs in private, voluntary associations, away from governments and therefore is not available to many who must deal with government, which include, especially, the poor.

Conservatives are wrong to abandon the public sector. Governments play essential roles, especially in relation to the disadvantaged, and governments are run by people – *by citizens* – who have the same needs as those citizens outside, in the private sector. They cannot be abandoned, no matter how dysfunctional they may seem in their low-grade depression, working in mechanical cultures.

Another reason we cannot abandon the government is addressed especially to conservatives. In wartime, even "conservative" governments, need to be "pro-government." We believe, in fact, that two important factors threatening the sustainability of a national commitment to 'the Long War' (desired by "order" conservatives) is the conservatives' 1) continuing opposition to government, in general, and 2) continuing efforts to undermine confidence in it on other, non-war-related issues.

If conservatives and Republicans want to lead in this war or any war (or, we would argue, if they want to govern effectively) they *need to become "pro-government."* They need to stop running away from government. To do this, conservatives will not, and should not, give up their traditional commitments to individualism, entrepreneurship, and decentralization. These values are crucial, not only for them, but also for any transpartisan vision for the nation and the world. To retain these values and assume a new pro-government posture, conservatives need to develop an active strategy for reforming government by promoting those same conservative values *inside the government.* Much of this essay describes how to do this, and the position is supported by many real examples and experiences.

Liberal attitudes toward government, too, are much more complicated than the current debate suggests. We have mentioned the "freedom" left's opposition to government encroachment on civil liberties. But even on issues relating to social welfare and concern for the disadvantaged, many liberals' support of government is not what it seems.

As we mentioned earlier, liberals do not necessarily like actual governments; they like mythical governments that behave as if they were guided by the liberal imagination. These mythical governments behave in ways that are totally different from the dysfunctional realities of actual governments. But, because the only thing liberals seem to dislike even more than actual governments is the conservatives' efforts to constrain governments, liberals may appear as irrational and incoherent. We think their position, as described above, is true in important respects. Conservatives think it is impossible to reform public schools, and they have simply given up trying. By letting people leave (through charter schools or vouchers), they believe at least they can save some of them, but their position does imply abandoning others, those "left behind," who are the most disadvantaged. Liberals can't accept that.

Conservatives and liberals agree that schools are in crisis. The only answer is to reform the schools. Unfortunately, neither side knows how to do this. Each side, in the current debate, is sacrificing one group of kids. When people leave the system, those left behind are sacrificed (by conservatives); without reform, those who could be saved by leaving are blocked from doing so (by liberals). Unfortunately, the debate can't get beyond the argument either to let children leave or force them to stay. The key to reform is to import private engagement into public schools and draw support from both conservatives and liberals. Models showing how to do this exist and can help guide reform initiatives.

To save the public sector, liberals need to join with conservatives to import into the government those elements of private, connected life that are essential to bringing out what is "human" in them. Liberals don't like bureaucracies any more than conservatives do. They need now to join forces in mitigating the brutalities of bureaucratic life so that everyone affected by them – people both inside and outside – can have a chance.

Ownership in Public Spaces

Ownership is essential to the transpartisan vision we are promoting. The Peruvian Hernando de Soto has become an international star in the development world by promoting private property rights in private spaces. At the end of 2007 he was actively working in about ten countries in all regions of the world. His vision is powerfully transpartisan, and his enthusiastic supporters span the political spectrum around the world. (Milton Friedman was a long-time supporter; Bill Clinton is currently de Soto's most famous major political advocate.)

Though de Soto promotes private rights in private space, our commitment to ownership focuses on creating *private rights* in *public spaces*. In these "public spaces" we include both bureaucratic, governmental institutions and large private corporations that are also bureaucratic and that also disempower people in them.

The "rights" we are advocating are not, of course, legal rights – though in some realms they can be made legal. The nature of these rights advances us again past the objective world of legal rights into the subjective world of informal, consensual rights. What such rights mean and how they work is obvious for anyone who has worked in an independent school or charter school. It is also perceptible in healthy public schools where everyone pitches in, works together to strengthen the school, and makes it as good as it can be.

We are talking about a model of cooperation that can be found everywhere in the private sector but not in many parts of the public one. We must transcend this current reality in favor of one that celebrates our "humanness" in all of life's experience — a reality that is truly transpartisan.

CHAPTER FOUR

NATIONAL SECURITY AND 'THE LONG WAR'

During a recent conference on Middle East peace, *New York Times* columnist Thomas L. Friedman noted that fear motivated most of the participants: Fatah's fear of Hamas, the Sunni countries' fear of Iran, and Israel's fear of Fatah's collapsing. In the United States, fear is the dominant influence driving the entire debate on foreign policy and national security, especially in dealing with the issue of terrorism.

There is much to fear in both the U.S. and other countries. It is thus not surprising that people everywhere devote huge efforts to preventing harm. The U.S. now spends as much on its military as the combined spending of most other countries.

We do not want to over-emphasize the issue of military spending because it is politically so contested at the present time. The threat of terrorism is still sufficient to limit opposition in the streets, as occurred during the Vietnam War, but opposition remains very deep. Although public surveys show that voters are deeply concerned about the issue, they widely perceive that the president's policy (the "surge") may be working. This has largely silenced the candidates running for the presidency in 2008, even the Democratic candidates.

Nevertheless, opposition remains alive on college campuses. Four thousand people signed a petition at Stanford to protest the Hoover Institution's recruitment of Donald Rumsfeld as a Distinguished Visiting Fellow. Many colleges continue their opposition to ROTC, opposition that began during the anti-war protests in the 1960s. This contention is a tragic symbol of political division that makes it difficult, if not impossible, for the country, which tends toward broad consensus on the war in Afghanistan and deep division on the war in Iraq, to pursue a serious, successful, integrated strategy on national security. This is especially true in our fight against terrorists, who, because they are unknown and distanced from states, are difficult if not impossible to deter. Even the nature of what challenges us remains contentious. Is fighting "terrorism" more like fighting Communism/Nazism or more like fighting Kamikaze airplanes?

The experiences in both Afghanistan and Iraq have revealed the limitations of military force when trying to engage nonstate adversaries. Passions run high on the issue of national security because the options seem so limited. In Iraq, the choice seemed to be between going to war and doing nothing. Some people might argue that "negotiation" or appeals to the United Nations offered a middle ground. But these middle ground options seem more fanciful than real — more like excuses for doing nothing. If no real options exist between the extremes of doing nothing and war, it is little wonder that people became polarized over the choice when so much seemed at stake.

From our transpartisan perspective, we are interested in exploring new strategies with great, potential strategic power that could both advance the larger objectives of U.S. foreign policy while appealing to conservatives and liberals alike. The problem in the current debate is that so little is understood or said about nonmilitary initiatives that could really make a difference in promoting change. As a result, we have little sense that one can do anything *positive* to make things better and really reduce the danger. This makes us even more fearful.

In the past, the focus of our foreign policy has been directed toward strong governments of strong nation-states.

Our principal adversaries — whether Nazi Germany, the Soviet Union, Communist China, or our enemies in World War I — all had strong governments that controlled their people and the range of issues that were important to them. Under the circumstances, foreign policy was directed entirely toward governments. In those times, all concern was focused on power, and the principal instruments of influence were coercive — rewarding friends and punishing enemies.

Since 9/11, we have come to recognize that we face an entirely new challenge. In the new reality, threats come primarily from a multitude of unknown, invisible nonstate actors (terrorists), who seek refuge in weak and fragile states. These weak states, which have very limited control over their societies or nonstate sectors, have now become the focus of our foreign policy. Apart from the state or government level, foreign policymakers must now pay close attention to changing perceptions and practices in the nonstate sector, where threats to Western and American security are developing.

This is a new challenge for foreign policy. Despite rhetoric to the contrary, foreign policymakers and the foreign policy community generally have not yet adjusted to the radically different requirements of foreign policy toward weak states. The substantial independence of societies within weak states render traditional foreign policy ineffective until foreign policymakers develop *distinct policies toward both states and societies.* Now they must understand and design policies that address *subjective* challenges in societies — challenges that include low levels of social trust, tribal social structures, and, often, huge internal conflict.

Lacking any such policies, the debate on foreign policy has simply pretended that weak states are strong — imagining they have the capacities necessary to do what we want from them. Such pretending leads to blaming them for their failure to perform and scolding them for either their weakness or their venality. This has been the story of the Israeli-Palestinian conflict for at least three decades, and it has been the central reality in our relationships with dictators in many places, especially in the Arab and Muslim countries. Since the only sin of the states we are scolding is that they are weak, these judgments — coming from conservatives and liberals alike — are useless at best and cruelly insensitive at worst, and only add to the widespread antipathy people in many parts of the world feel toward us.[1]

Lacking separate policies toward societies, policymakers left to deal only with states either assert strongly hawkish policies (conservatives) or extremely passive policies combined with appeals to international organizations (liberals), and the options considered are artifacts dredged up from the past experience dealing with strong states. Both conservatives and liberals see one another's limitations, and both are right. We need something entirely new that both sides will support.

In order to develop strategies and policies toward societies, it is first necessary to understand them and the special issues that arise when nonstate sectors pose challenges to weak states.

One of the most important attributes of societies within weak states is a *lack of social trust*, which inhibits both economic and political development, and is linked to the lack of political cohesion and consensus essential to democracy. Lack of social trust limits people's ability to do business impersonally, which, along with property rights, is crucial to the growth of firms and, therefore, to economic development. This explains the internal conflict that can be found in many weak states — conflict that results from powerful sub-loyalties of tribe, ethnic group, and religious belief, which weak states cannot transcend.

In designing policy for the nonstate, society sector, policymakers must focus on strengthening civil society in ways that promote economic, political, and social change. The most challenging task will be to promote social trust and reduce internal conflict, thereby giving existing regimes a better chance to function and survive. This is a subject too large to explore in depth in this essay. However, there is a large and growing body of both theory and real experiences in creating models of success using civil society initiatives to promote change in a variety of different social areas. These include promoting economic development, girls' education and women's empowerment, peace, democracy and infrastructure in societies, both during and after conflicts.[2]

Strengthening civil societies will start to promote active, engaged strategies for bringing together people who are now in conflict. It will start to build trust and hope not only between people in conflict in countries outside the United States, but inside the United States, as well.

Two other issues in the national security area are ripe for transpartisan attention: first is improving law enforcement and recruiting citizens in support of homeland security; and second is the issue of spending for security.

Improved Law Enforcement and Recruitment of Citizens

On August 15, 2006, George Will, a dean of conservative American pundits, wrote an article in *The Washington Post*, concluding that the London plot to blow up planes leaving Heathrow Airport and bound for the U.S. demonstrated that improved law enforcement, "which probably could have prevented Sept. 11," is crucial to combating terrorism. "F-16s," he wrote, "are not useful tools against terrorism that issues from places such as Hamburg (where Mohamed Atta lived before dying in the North Tower of the World Trade Center) and High Wycombe, England."

Since 9/11, our political leaders, starting with the president, have led a massive initiative to strengthen domestic security. The initiative included the formation of a celebrated presidential commission, enormous governmental reorganization, and creation of the Department of Homeland Security. A cynic might say that the *theater* of effective action has been brilliant – worthy of Cecil B. de Mille in his prime.

The blizzard of activity on behalf of domestic security has focused almost entirely on mechanical responses to various threats: the searches at airports, development of space-age technologies for detecting contraband, domestic wiretaps – and the rest of it – all while a country that should be united in confronting the threat is being torn apart by it. This is because our policy-makers have made no effort whatsoever to recruit citizens as active partners in building security. Just as foreign policy has no role for citizens and bases all policy on pretending weak governments are strong, our current government thinks it can do it alone and that technology is all the government needs to make us secure.

There can be no security as long as our politics is as divided as it is and as long as citizens are not actively recruited as partners in promoting security. The general conflict in our politics militates against where we need to be. It is impossible to imagine how we might develop such a united commitment as long as our leaders continue to see each other as embodiments of evil. We have emphasized the need to promote social trust in the weak states that have become the new challenges to our security, but our own domestic security depends on embracing that very same objective in our own country. Security depends on promoting trust by creating venues for people to communicate across loyalties, and do it on a very large scale.

Spending for Security

Some liberals believe that the principal reason for conservative support for military spending is that it is good for the economy. Let us dispense with this view at the outset: military spending is a cost; it is not a benefit except to the extent it provides a real contribution to security. Beyond that, military spending is waste.

Two spending issues lend themselves to transpartisan consideration. First are general levels of spending for weapons versus other activities that will increase security. At current levels, something like ninety-five percent of total spending for security is directed toward the military. Only five percent is being spent on nonmilitary activities. If foreign policy were still (as in the past) focused entirely on states, these might be reasonable allocations. However, the new challenges we face from weak states and the need to engage their *societies* suggest we need to rethink this ratio and devote much more than we do now to the nonmilitary side. The problem is that just as our government has no sense of how to design and implement civil society initiatives to promote change in societies, it also lacks the capacity to spend money in ways that would strategically support the new policies that are needed. This is a large subject that needs very serious attention.[3]

The second spending issue is about spending for particular weapons. We are not experts on this subject, but we understand the logic of spending decisions made in response to political lobbying rather than strategic concerns. We also know experts we trust who can cite many examples of weapons systems that are generations better than the weapons of any possible adversary, and therefore do not need further development. Addressing these issues seriously will be important especially as part of a "grand bargain" between left and right on entitlements spending.

Our final comment on this point must sound a note of caution about rushing to spend money on nonmilitary projects. Until we have a much clearer sense of an appropriate strategy and until we develop capacities to spend money more strategically, we should shy away from proposals to increase spending quickly. Developing the appropriate strategy requires the broad, committed participation of the American people.

*   *   *

By choosing to include policy toward 'the Long War' in our list of potential transpartisan issues, we are not claiming to know a specific policy that would be successful or attract transpartisan support in all of its dimensions. Our burden is much simpler and easier: it is to sketch *parts* of foreign and national security policy that could attract transpartisan support and stimulate a collaboration between government and the citizens it represents. If we could initiate a collaborative process to begin developing transpartisan policies, it would encourage a promotion of trust that would resonate throughout our national security community as well as our political system in general.

CHAPTER FIVE

CHALLENGES OF AN UNCONNECTED SOCIETY:
RACE, SEXUAL PREFERENCE, AND RELIGION

As is the case for relationships in the Middle East, domestic social issues such as race, sexual preference and religion are contentious because all are grounded in fear. Fear exists on both sides of every issue: minorities fearing the white majority, the white majority fearing minorities; gays fearing straights, and straights fearing gays; and secular and religious people fearing each other.

It is interesting that none of these issues is currently in play in our political debate. Although they are "public issues," no major political figure has action proposals or even, aside from Barack Obama's speeches on race, much to say about how we might solve or mitigate them. Understanding this silence will create important background to explore what might be done to make a real difference.

Consider, for example, our nation's experience with "desegregation." The school desegregation cases began when the Supreme Court's 1954 decision in *Brown v. Board of Education* first mandated desegregation of public schools,[1] and it led to widespread "bussing" as a means of forcing integration. Although mainstream liberal organizations like the civil rights groups and the American Civil Liberties Union continue to support integration through bussing, schools are today more separated than ever in many places, and hope has largely been drained from the belief that bussing can achieve integration. Forced integration of the schools by bussing children far from their homes was controversial from the beginning, even among many African-American parents who voted Democratic and considered themselves liberals.

Even where integration was "achieved," the results were often unreal. In most cases, "integrated schools" were actually *internally segregated*, with continuing racial tension and little evidence of racial collaboration. The objective of any integration policy should be an embracing of openness between and among all groups who are "different." Bussing could not, and cannot, achieve that goal. So, in June 2007, when the Supreme Court reversed the integration requirement — an event that went largely unnoticed — what had been the centerpiece of civil rights action for more than three decades was abandoned![2]

These issues have been essentially erased from political discourse because the public policy initiatives mandated by governments devoid of citizen involvement have, in large part, failed. For solutions, we need to look in other places.

The current debate on these issues defined largely by fear limits the universe of remedies to mechanistic appeals to legal rights, with each side claiming "rights" against the other. Settling competing claims of right requires the use of force to enforce the rights claimed. To search for real solutions that reduce fear, promote acceptance, encourage respect, and enable real integration of people of different races and religions, we must look beyond unconnected mechanisms to strategies for organically engaging and connecting people. To learn how we might actually do this, we must observe where it's actually being done, such as inner-city parochial schools (see Chapter Two) and in particular communities, such as Oak Park, Illinois, an inner ring suburb on the west side of Chicago that began its four-decade commitment to real integration in the late 1960s.[3]

Rethinking the Relationships
How does the political system understand the relationships between people — between people of different races, religions, and sexual preferences? The public/legal institutions say

that, implicitly, they have no relationships at all – zero. Their relationships are defined only by respective rights that external force can impose on them.

Claims of right-demanding external behaviors exist only in the *objective* world – *in public*. While this can be important for groups oppressed by public institutions and laws (such as the laws requiring blacks to sit in the back of Southern buses before the Civil Rights Movement), it does nothing to cure the subjective, private rejection that can be just as painful as external discrimination. No claim of right can compel *subjective* acceptance and force people to honor one another, which is deeply important to most people. Without such acceptance, "disadvantaged," "discriminated against" groups can feel fatally wounded and resentful.

For a time, people thought politically correct language could solve the problem of personal relationships. Political correctness is a small-minded practice – sold as the highest form of idealism but animated by shame – that thinks it is humane to pretend people are what they are not. In this worldview short people are "vertically challenged" and the handicapped are "physically challenged." This kind of political correctness has now largely disappeared, but the reason, again, shows the bankruptcy of our political debate and language.

Intimate, accepting relationships between people of different race, sexual preference, and religion can only be achieved through personal engagement and connection – principles that are central to our vision of a transpartisan politics. This is why the mechanistic remedies, responding to claims of legal right, *in practice* separate people and retard development of engaged, connected relationships that would substantially solve these troublesome issues.

We think the life story of John Callahan, the quadriplegic cartoonist who became a hero to the handicapped by poking fun at them, illustrates crucial points central to understanding transpartisan citizenship. Callahan became famous by creating cartoons like the one depicting a posse surrounding a wheelchair with the caption, "Don't worry, he won't get far on foot."

In his book *The Winner Within*, NBA Coach Pat Riley writes: "Callahan's humor… offends some people, but lots of others — especially among the forty-three million Americans who are classified as handicapped — find that something liberating happens when you laugh about your adversities. One of his extended pieces is even called *'The Lighter Side of Being Paralyzed for Life.'* He'd rather turn painful situations into jokes than be indulged by a pitying, patronizing attitude."[4]

The website selling Callahan's latest book says: "This book is not for the timid, the easily offended, the politically correct, or your grandparents."

As important as the objective rights to free speech and individual self-identity are, a far more powerful concern propelling the resistance to "political correctness," in our view, was the subjective impact this language was having on its supposed *beneficiaries*: the objectively identified "underdog" groups.

Pretending that someone who is handicapped is not says, in effect, that handicaps are so terrible, the only way we can deal with them is to not deal with them at all — pretend they do not exist. Politically correct language creates an artificial *public* relationship that conflicts absolutely with the individuals' *private self-conception*. This is a grotesque way of refusing to accept people as they are. It fails to embrace them as they see themselves. For this reason AIDS activists in the 1980s and '90s worked hard to change media references to them as "AIDS victims" to "people with AIDS."

Politically correct formulations are powerful examples of the mechanical worldview, which underlies the partisan political dynamic, displacing the organic world experience. They are an example of the external public arena trumping the inner subjective essence of individual self that animates life. John

Callahan truly highlighted the "winner within" by the way he resisted a pitying, patronizing attitude and took reality in stride with both humor and skill. This behavior underscores the essential attributes of a transpartisan world. John Callahan became a hero to people with handicaps because he removed the shame that is still implicit in politically correct language.

Because of ridicule by both conservative and liberal critics, and the inherent insensitivity to the right of self-identification, political correctness has now largely disappeared.

The intimate, personal nature of relationships involving race, sexual preference, religion and other such associations can only be affirmed by the engaged, connected interactions that are central to transpartisan politics. The lack of intimacy and subjectivity in mechanistic remedies based solely on claims of legal rights separates people, rather than bringing them together, and suppresses the engaged, connected relationships that would substantially reduce the public tension associated with these intimate matters.

Responsibilities freely chosen and accepted are more likely to be honored than responsibilities imposed. While this may sound like a prescription for doing nothing, we *should* be asking the question: what stimulates a sense of obligation to strangers – to people not in one's "tribe"? The answer is: *personal engagement*. Personal engagement, encouraged by communication across loyalties, first promotes trust, then deeper relationships, then real connection, and finally love. These are qualities that are alien from the mechanistic policy-making that dominates our mainstream political debate, on the left as well as the right.

These issues bring into play one of the most important challenges underlying our view of a transpartisan politics: the creation of engaged and connected institutions, both public and private.

Standing in the way of justice for "oppressed groups" are *perceptions* of private rejection, whether real or not. For example, we are convinced that a major impetus behind the rise in popularity of fundamentalist religion is the pain and anger induced by the rejection by secularists and more conventional religionists. When "outsiders" are rejected by the dominant social group, it causes them pain and spawns resentment and rebellion.

Although oppressed groups are championed primarily by the political left, the point we are making is not just aimed at the left. The political left has traditionally responded by promoting material equality. If public acceptance, however, comes at the price of private rejection, pain will persist and sometimes assume more intense forms.

Race

Race remains an enormous issue in America. Yet until the 2008 Presidential election, active debate about it over the past two decades has all but disappeared in the American political debate. The issue reappeared when an African-American became the surprising front-runner for the Democratic presidential nomination. However, the public debate focused only on issues relating to Obama's electability (*e.g.*, his association with Rev. Wright), not on real issues that need real attention.

One among many indicators of the continuing struggle of race is the fact that there are today only half as many young black men in college as young black women. What, if anything, can the assertion of legal rights do to solve this problem? Some liberals thought the answer was affirmative action. Others, including some liberals and probably most conservatives, supported Bill Cosby in his widely publicized efforts to get black leaders to take responsibility for the serious social problems that persist among black youth. He was shouted down and condemned in the strongest terms by liberal and civil rights groups, who accused him of failing to acknowledge the continuing effects of white racism.

It is hard to avoid the conclusion that at the heart of blacks' continuing struggle is their victim identity. In his book on the crisis in the black culture, *Enough*, National Public Radio senior correspondent Juan Williams exposes the corrosive effect of blacks' victim identity. Citing the fact that black kids who try to get good grades are often accused of "acting like Whitey," Williams argues that "many African-American leaders have lost touch with a hallmark of the civil rights movement — the tradition of self-empowerment. Instead, they've embraced the notion of 'victimhood'."[5]

"I think it's a terrible signal to our young people... to have black leadership that in a knee-jerk fashion defends negative, dysfunctional behavior," Williams concludes.

The most terrible, crippling aspect of victim identity is *conceptual*. When you say that any group is an inherent victim, victimized by another group's hostility (*e.g.*, white racism), you are asserting that the victim group has no control over its own destiny. Belief that blacks are inherent victims explains why individual blacks who claim to be successful are often attacked as "Uncle Toms" or "house slaves"[6] — successful only because they sold out. In the 2008 Democratic presidential primaries, Bill and Hillary Clinton contributed, probably inadvertently, to this line of argument when they suggested that Barack Obama is an elitist. This disparagement of success is a subtlety crippling form of racism that occurs too often in the mainstream debate on race. The continuing challenge of race fifty years after *Brown v. Board of Education* is manifest in the persistence of blacks' victim identity. This, we believe, is what underlies the nihilism and celebration of despair that Juan Williams and Bill Cosby have tried to confront. Cosby's rebuke by civil rights leaders, who accused him of not understanding the depth of white racism, is the classic posture of victim identity.

Can anything be done about this? Almost four decades ago, Daniel Patrick Moynihan said the best medicine for the problem of race in America was — his famous phrase — "benign neglect." We have now had four decades of it, with what result? The debate is caught between one side (civil rights leaders and many of the left generally) that argues blacks can do nothing until whites change and racism disappears, and the other side (conservatives and some liberals) that says the ball is in the blacks' court, and they need to take responsibility for their own problems. One side says all power lies with whites, and the other says blacks have all the power they need to alter their situation.

The issue of race and other problems is now — we believe — largely about how citizens engage and treat each other. It is about *relationships* between people, which are greatly influenced by the structure of institutions and by leadership. Policymaking that tries to reconcile races by mechanistic reliance on bussing or affirmative action alone (i.e., by moving bodies around) inhibits the personal engagement that is the key to solving this problem. Personal engagement, sustained by institutionalizing communication across loyalties, is the key to ending both white racism and perceptions of white racism. It is the key to raising positive symbols of possibility for black males now influenced by the often destructive nihilism of the rapper culture. Finally, it is the key to ending the tragic legacy of slavery, which still encourages many black Americans — with notable exceptions in entertainment, sports, and a growing black middle class — to feel like second-class citizens.

We want here to proffer a transpartisan diagnosis and cure: The problem is not primarily one of "white racism," which by every measure has declined enormously over the past five decades. The problem is a by-product, rather, *of an unengaged society* in which *people do not "see" African-Americans*. This is not a result of Ralph Ellison's (*The Invisible Man*) belief that blacks are invisible because they are black. The reason is because *an unengaged society does not "see" anyone outside one's own group.* And, to everyone's detriment, our so-called "public" institutions make no real effort to engage people and encourage them to "see" each other by communicating across loyalties.

Gender and Sexual Preference

Justice Lewis Powell provided the deciding fifth vote in the 1988 case of *Bowers v. Hardwick*, denying the right of privacy to gay individuals. Two years later he expressed public regret for his decision. A decade and a half later the Supreme Court overturned the case by a six to three vote.

"I don't believe I've ever met a homosexual," Powell told one of his law clerks at the time of *Bowers*. The clerk, who in fact was gay, said, "Certainly you have, but you just don't know that they are."[7] (The gay clerk, whom Justice Powell addressed when he said he had never met a homosexual, later argued the case *Lawrence v. Texas*, before the Supreme Court, which overturned Powell's regretful *Bowers* decision.)

This story, now something of a legend in the gay community, highlights one aspect of the complicated relationship between public acceptance and private rejection – or at least the *fear* of it. Powell's clerk had an opportunity to reveal his "secret" but chose not to. The reason, presumably, was fear of rejection, were his secret to become public. In a more open, engaged culture, he would have felt safer.

The importance of *private* connections in *public* policy also played a role in another important Supreme Court case, also involving the traditionally conservative Justice Powell. He provided the key vote and wrote the opinion in *Roe v. Wade*, based partly on his personal experience counseling a young man in a situation that involved a woman who died obtaining an illegal abortion.

We are not denying that problems of rights remain in regard to gays or blacks. The right to marry is obviously a very important issue for gays who wish to externalize their commitments in formal, legal ways, and it will remain a serious issue until this right is achieved equally, everywhere. We do not claim that any transpartisan measure for increasing engagement and connection among gay and straight people will achieve broad support for gay marriage anytime soon.[8] We do, however, argue three things: first, that private, subjective acceptance is important to most if not all gays — as it is to blacks and to practically everybody — independent of legal rights; second, that substantial efforts to promote personal engagement between gay and straight people will in powerful ways promote acceptance, trust, and even love between them; and third, that increasing private acceptance, while not necessarily reducing opposition to gay marriage, will increase support for formal validation of the loving personal relationships formed among all individuals, regardless of gender or sexual preference.

It is no secret that the greatest conflict surrounding gay rights lies in the "red" portion of certain states, where there are the fewest opportunities for engagement between gay and straight people. While this fact makes it more difficult to imagine a solution to this problem than for problems of race, there is little question that personal engagement is the solution to "humanizing" relationships on this issue, as well.

Religion/Spirituality

Now we address the most conflicted issue of all: religion and the related issue of spirituality. The great puzzle is this: how, at the same time, can religion inspire some people to attain the highest moments of love and acceptance of one another, while it also inspires others to engage in the most brutal conflict, driven by blind rage? Even when formal religion is not involved, quasi-religious totalitarian political systems appealing to religious longing — whether of left or right — attain levels of brutality that are beyond comprehension and often far exceed the brutality that occurs where religion is not involved. Rousseau characterized the "idealism" in totalitarian brutality in his famous statement:

"We must 'force men to be free.'" The horrors done in the name of the 'good' (or God) continue, to this day. The horrors happen not despite their quasi-religious quality, but often because of it.

How can we create a transpartisan approach to religion and spirituality? The challenge is to identify issues on which traditional, practicing religious people – who belong to formal religious institutions – share common concerns with people whose devotional practices are less formal (or not formal at all) but are nevertheless spiritual.

The so-called "Establishment Clause" in the First Amendment to the Constitution requires the separation of church and state. In the past half-century, the courts have interpreted the clause as requiring absolute exclusion of both religion and spirituality from public institutions. The impact of this has been greatest in the schools, whose entire curriculum and culture have been governed by a rigid, mechanistic worldview. As a result, we have replaced one set of formal religious ceremonies (that some believe are empty, but are essentially innocuous) with a brutal "civic" religion without spirit, which philosophically acts every bit as much like a religion as does Christianity, Judaism, or Islam. In practice, this "civic" religion is largely responsible for creating the disturbing, desperate, nightmare cultures in many public schools, which – deprived of spirit – are therefore also not *human*. To think that the Establishment Clause requires excluding spirit from classrooms is to think that it requires excluding everything *human* from classrooms. No word is strong enough to describe the tragedy that has resulted – all in the name of the highest idealism, as interpreted by the highest court in the land. What the court has given us is life without life... in a word: death.

The courts' interpretation of the Establishment Clause not only has little to do with what the Founding Fathers had in mind when they wrote the clause; it is the very opposite of what everyone in education – and everyone outside it who is alive – wants education to be, and knows it must be, to begin to succeed in any meaningful way.

We believe the courts have played an extraordinarily negative role in promoting the mechanistic view of people that lies at the heart of our disengaged society. However, they have tried, recently, to undo some of the damage. A recent case has permitted moments of nonsectarian silence and the use of school grounds for personal, private religious and spiritual meetings. Here, the court has tried to broaden the space for personal engagement and ameliorate the bureaucratic deadness that dominates our public schools.

Just as the bureaucratic state is dead, bureaucratic religion can also become dead and thus deaden those subject to its power. We do not claim any knowledge of how and where religious rituals lose their spiritual quality and become mechanical. But it can happen, and the results scale hideous heights when people start killing each other in the name of religion.

The transpartisan question regarding public spirituality, like so much else at the societal bedrock, is how can public spaces be opened and their mechanical cultures transformed to allow spirit into them so that they can be alive? How can this be done without allowing those very opportunities for spirit to be turned into empty ceremonies in which every student is asked, for the sake of conformity, to put a pinch of incense on the altar of religion?

Creating public spaces for private engagement that enliven our fragmented and dying public institutions is the central mission of transpartisan policies.

Part III

The Transpartisan Imperative

One hundred and thirty million Americans remain outside the partisan political world defined by the country's two major political parties. Fifty-five million register as independents or members of third parties, and another seventy-five million do not register at all. An increasing number of registered partisans are growing restless with the ideological confines of their parties. These groups, together, comprise a powerful, new political constituency, potentially larger than the 125 million that voted for president in 2004. Raising money through the Internet creates a powerful potential for funding this constituency.[1]

The current partisan system marginalizes one-half of potential voters who are either unaffiliated or alienated from the two "major" political parties. It traps politicians and constituents alike in endless peripheral bickering that relies on fear to exploit artificial divisions between various shades of "conservatives" and "liberals." This focus on conflict allows partisans to win by the numbers — elections, legislative floor votes, polls — without effectively engaging large portions of the nation's people. No wonder, as we are writing, public confidence in the president is historically low and public confidence in Congress is even lower.

A transpartisan politics offers the chance to break the gridlock, moving beyond the fear-based, mechanistic divisiveness of current politics. It is an opportunity to create hopeful, organic approaches to issues, with strong citizen participation, focusing on initiatives based on collaboration.

In this section we say why a transpartisan politics is an imperative for us at the present moment in history. We believe this impulse was an important factor in the founding of the American republic. It was also very evident in the period immediately after 9/11, when people came together in powerful common purpose and no one questioned that citizens needed to partner with the government to respond to a crisis that is ongoing.

CHAPTER SIX

A CALL TO ACTION:
THE TRANSPARTISAN OPPORTUNITY

The transpartisan impulse has two themes, one substantive and other instrumental. The instrumental or process theme calls for a new public conversation that moves beyond polarization and brings people together through facilitated dialogue, deliberation, and conflict resolution. The process is about *personal engagement* – nothing very complicated, just people working together, engaging each other, without the highly moralistic demonizing that animates so much of our current mainstream political and intellectual debates. Barack Obama has championed this style of politics more than any of the candidates in the 2008 presidential election so far. It is interesting that the Republican who most exemplifies transpartisan qualities, John McCain, secured the Republican nomination as his party's candidate.

The substantive side of transpartisanship is also important. As of this writing, both Obama and McCain appear politically vulnerable because neither has a substantive, transpartisan program.

With engagement comes *trust* – the essential glue that makes almost everything possible and without which almost nothing works. Trust eliminates the sense that the future is threatened by demons on "the other side." It opens spaces to see truths across political divides, truths that unite people who are now locked in frantic conflict. They are truths that have a chance to solve real problems.

The substantive element in transpartisanship is related to the instrumental. It focuses on active citizenship and citizen engagement as crucial, now largely ignored, elements in solving problems ranging from the crisis in public schools to the new, post-9/11 challenges facing foreign policy. Transpartisan thinking insists that expanded political debate and governance structures include significant spaces for active participation by citizens. When issues require citizen participation, citizens also need to be included in designing policy positions.

The importance of citizens is obvious enough for people outside the government — people who do not work for the government — but *we also need to engage citizens inside governments, who need to see their responsibilities in new ways.*

The most visible self-identified transpartisan organization in the United States today, Reuniting America, which we serve as advisors, has since its founding in 2003, held dozens of meet-ings that bring together people associated with groups across the political spectrum — groups with a collective membership of more than thirty million. (See Appendix for listing of groups whose leaders attended Reuniting America transpartisan policy meetings)

Over the past three years, such politically diverse figures as former Vice President Al Gore; conservative activist and president of *Americans for Tax Reform*, Grover Norquist; former conservative congressman, Bob Barr; former president of *Common Cause*, Chellie Pingree; co-founder of the liberal group *MoveOn.org*, Joan Blades; and head of the *Christian Coalition*, Roberta Combs, have participated in Reuniting America meetings on issues as wide-ranging as energy and environmental policy, American policy toward Iran, the future of women in politics, and the future of the Internet .

The challenge facing Reuniting America, as for anyone committed to a transpartisan politics, is to search for issues and approaches that bring people together to do what they agree about. One of our purposes here is to shine a light in places often overlooked, places that now seem beyond reach, but which become possible through collaboration and co-creation of solutions. The approaches we describe are not dreams unconnected to reality; they are based on real experiences.

Transpartisanship describes collaborative efforts among citizens and political leaders who focus on the importance of active citizenship and public-private partnerships. Transpartisanship makes it possible to achieve the ideals of a democratic republic by integrating the values of a democracy – freedom, equality, and a regard for the common good – with the values of a republic – order, responsibility, and security.

Transpartisanship is, in its nature, an evolving concept – in constant development and refinement, with ongoing citizen engagement. Static debate, in which positions never change, happen when there is no engagement – when there is no life in the political process. This is largely where we are today, with different positions often more determined by certainty about what to oppose than what to embrace. (Recall the discussion in Chapter One on the unresolved conflicts between the freedom and order constituencies within both the left and the right.)

The transpartisan impulse is largely about integrating diversity. The glue that holds them together is civic engagement and the social trust it promotes. This essay is filled with examples of how "conservatives" and "liberals" who are lost in conflict in the larger debate – when they are fighting over large, abstract issues of government without any role for individual citizens or communities – can come together in common purpose as citizens working with governments to solve public issues.

The philosophical underpinnings of the transpartisan impulse may be found in the writings of Thomas Hobbes, John Locke, Adam Smith, and the Scottish Enlightenment thinkers; and this impulse played an important role in the founding of the American democratic republic.

Addressing the Nature of Life: Nasty, Brutish, and Short

The core concepts of the American constitutional task – all persons are equal; each has rights to life and liberty; governments are created by the people to ensure security and contentment among people – are based on natural law. In his 1651 book *Leviathan*, Thomas Hobbes laid the foundation for modern democracy in explaining the need for governments: to soften the harshness of the natural world (in which the life of man is "solitary, poor, nasty, brutish, and short"), provide security, and ensure their natural right to live free.

From John Locke the American founders committed to an educated citizenry as the key to a thriving polity, and they added "the greatest happiness for the greatest number" from the Scottish Enlightenment. Both Hobbes and the Scottish Enlightenment philosophers thought the Golden Rule offered the best chance for people to get what they wanted: to treat others as they want to be treated. At the heart of both the American cultural and political experiences was the idea that avoiding a nasty and brutish life would result from being happy and from making others happy.

The architects of the American Revolution drew on these ideas in creating the unique American intertwining of freedom and order that was their antidote to the terrors of anarchy and tyranny on sharp display during the French Revolution.

The intertwined subjective values and material objectives that have shaped the unfolding American story rest on a continuing set of transpartisan impulses. They call on "conservative" and "liberal" sensibilities the way walking requires integrating the action of the left leg and the right. They rest on the recognition that security and freedom need each other for either to be achieved. We call these impulses the Transpartisan Imperative.

The Founding

The transpartisan impulse of integrating diversity fueled the American Revolution and allowed a politically marginalized constituency of American colonists to transform the British colonies in America into the United States of America. The founding of the American republic can be seen as the beginning of the history of transpartisan politics, as it promoted a politics, in Lincoln's famous phrase, "of the people, by the people, for the people." Public life, this observation declares, is not only about governments; it also includes *people*.

The American adventure with powerful democratic institutions began in 1765, when American colonial leaders convened a continental congress in New York City to protest the British Stamp Act. This act was the first British tax on the American colonies since their establishment 150 years earlier. During this Stamp Act Congress, the colonies for the first time expressed a united position and demanded their English rights. They objected to "taxation without representation." Parliament repealed the Stamp Act, but it was too late. Over the next twenty-five years, the American colonists held two more Continental Congresses, declared their independence, and held a Congress of the Confederation and a Constitutional Convention. They fought a successful war against England, drafted and ratified a Constitution, and in December 1791, adopted a Bill of Rights, completing their political organizing project.

This quarter century laid the foundation for the American democratic republic. It was a transpartisan event because it brought together disparate people into unity, and also because it insisted on including the people in its conception of "public." The commitment to transpartisanship was imperative because integrating diversity, that is, both freedom and order, were essential to the survival of the American experiment in democracy.

Forming a More Perfect Union

In *The Federalist Papers* James Madison and Alexander Hamilton both advocated a transpartisan politics when they wrote against factions.[1] Madison lists "complaints" against factions that read like today's disgust with partisan politics. People of all political hues, he wrote, complain that governments are too unstable, and that "the public good is disregarded in the conflicts of rival parties." They also complain that public decisions are too often decided not by appealing to justice and the rights of minority parties, "but by the superior force of an interested and over-bearing majority..." The problem, he said, is caused by "a factious spirit."

To control factions, Hamilton described new governance tools in the Constitution, including: "the regular distribution of power into distinct departments; the introduction of legislative balances and checks; the institution of courts composed of judges holding their offices during good behavior; the representation of the people in the legislature by deputies of their own election..." with "certain... power[s]" left to the states.

The Federalist Papers project itself serves as a kind of transpartisan model. Hamilton wrote as the foremost spokesman for the centralizing Federalists. Madison acted as the voice of decentralization and advocate of states rights and individual freedom. Together they supported the new constitution, which was a statement from "We the people..."

In an important sense, the founders were dealing with an easier, simpler time — a country of three million people held together by strong shared social, cultural, and religious values. However much they worried about faction, the pull of division and conflict was less then than it is today. Their institutional innovations, reducing division, focused on retarding precipitous action and government abuse of citizens' rights. Many more factors promote conflict today — thus the special emphasis we place on a strong concept of citizenship, which was strong at the time of the founding and has grown weak. While preventing government abuse of citizens' rights remains important, we must meet even larger challenges in the task of unifying our diverse people today.

The Structure: Congress Shall Make No Law

Hamilton, the centralizer, was concerned about order. The Constitution addressed the problem of anarchy — the problem of order. No more mobs would roam the countryside. Madison, the decentralizer, was concerned about freedom and preventing abuse of governmental powers, hence the separation of powers and the division of power between the states and the national government. To prevent governmental abuse, Madison also campaigned for the Bill of Rights.

Although faction is in our nature, we argue that *the impulse to cooperation and connection is also in our nature.* We believe that the more opportunities we give people to engage and connect with each other, the more they will mitigate the effects of faction. The more people can fulfill their desires, reach their goals, and win their personal life contests by cooperation, the less they will rely on factions and conflict to "get all they can."

Americans today experience the factions the founders were concerned about as pernicious partisan paralysis. Today's partisan problem is caused by both ideology and institutional structure. Ideologically, it is rooted in our political spectrum, seen as a continuum from left to middle to right — a narrow statement of possibilities that greatly limits our political debate and our political options.

We need to account for the conflict between freedom and order within both the left and the right. This points to a four-quadrant matrix (order-right, freedom-right, order-left, and freedom-left) which is far more descriptive of American politics from its inception to now. Integration of these four positions is the central purpose of the transpartisan imperative.

Institutionally, exclusion of citizens both inside and outside the government from effective participation in public business disempowers everyone and converts political debate into zero-sum game arguments about the government. No wonder there is so much conflict in politics seen this way.

The Transpartisan Context: We Are All Republicans, We Are All Federalists

Each of the three formative documents of the United States — the Declaration of Independence, the Constitution, and the Bill of Rights — represents a different aspect of the four-part matrix. Jefferson drafted the Declaration as a thrust for freedom. In today's world, both freedom-left and freedom-right actors embrace Jeffersonian democracy. The Constitution, heavily influenced by Hamiltonian federalism, focused on order, supported today by order advocates on both the left and right. The Bill of Rights followed the Constitution as freedom's repost. Both values — freedom and order — are essential for all modern people, because freedom without order is anarchy, and order without freedom is tyranny.

Jefferson underscored the transpartisan nature of the founding generation in his First Inaugural Address in the following words: "[E]very difference of opinion is not a difference of principle. We have called by different names brethren of the same principle. We are all Republicans, we are all Federalists." He then embraced opponents of the enterprise in a powerfully transpartisan spirit: "If there be any among us who would wish to dissolve this Union or to change its republican form, let them stand undisturbed as monuments of the safety with which error of opinion may be tolerated where reason is left free to combat it."

While the founders worked away at their political task, a second front for individual freedom and democratic order opened up in England, especially in Adam Smith's writing about the foundations of a moral order (in *The Theory of Moral Sentiments*, written in 1759) and the importance of free economic markets (in *The Wealth of Nations*, written in 1776).

Smith's argument for the liberating power of free markets paralleled Jefferson's argument for democratic political power vested in "the people." Both argued that power flowed up from the people rather than down from the leaders and that followers empowered leaders.

In the Civil War the young republic was once again challenged to produce unity from diversity. For the purpose of reconciliation, Lincoln reached back to the Declaration of Independence — putting the origin of the nation at 1776 rather than 1789, the year of the Constitution — and put the central authority for our democracy in the people. In the Gettysburg Address, he called on the nation to give "a new birth of freedom." His call was an imperative, ensuring survival of the "government of the people, by the people, for the people."

Doris Kearnes Goodwin, in *Team of Rivals*, her Pulitzer Prize-winning biography of Lincoln, captures the spirit of his governing above factions. Lincoln chose for his cabinet each of his rivals from his party for the presidency; and when he gave his Second Inaugural Address, the audience included his Vice President Andrew Johnson, a union-supporting Democrat from a slave-holding state.[2]

Lincoln tied together the impulse that saved the union in his Second Inaugural in the following, famous words: "With malice toward none; with charity for all; with firmness in the right, as God gives us to see the right, let us strive on to finish the work we are in; to bind up the nation's wounds; to care for him who shall have borne the battle, and for his widow, and his orphan — to do all which may achieve and cherish a just and lasting peace, among ourselves, and with all nations."

We had fought a terrible civil war. Yet we were *together*. Now, in his words, we needed "to finish the work we are in." The work remains unfinished even today. The transpartisan agenda shows how to finish it.

The unfinished mechanistic objectives of citizenship that lay at the heart of the Civil War disappeared from the legal structure of the Union with the adoption of the Civil War amendments to the Constitution. The Thirteenth Amendment abolished slavery. The Fourteenth Amendment, the Great Amendment, banned state laws denying people equal protection of the laws. And the Fifteenth protected the right to vote.

These are the constitutional and legal protections. The transpartisan challenge today is to extend the *spirit* of these protections to all Americans and to all people.

Transpartisan Discourse

To create a transpartisan politics, it is first important to expand political discourse. American politics is currently understood within extremely narrow boundaries — the left/right continuum, stylized sound-bite "debates," the expectation of sustained consistency over a political career, and party loyalty. New ideas are forced to remain close to the conventional wisdom, as the system marginalizes politicians who make excessively innovative proposals. A central challenge, of course, is to maintain stability while also promoting innovation.

The prison and penal reform discussion in Chapter Two suggests an important transpartisan innovation for introducing new ideas into the policy debate. Citizens simply start *doing* something, bringing together all major elements in a community; then look for funding to support it, perhaps first private and, later, public funding. Nothing written in the stars says that new ideas can come only from elected representatives. In fact, elected representatives may be effectively blocked from creating and/or embracing many innovative ideas. The penal example shows that the number of committed citizens doesn't have to be very great. And even if public funding is not available to support it, the Internet offers a huge pool of new funding to support new ideas.

As they begin to proliferate, these groups could borrow from the American revolutionary experience the role of the Committees of Correspondence, with each group informing the others of their latest efforts. (There are, in fact, several parallels between today's transpartisan constituency and the American colonists marginalized by the King's government.)

Innovative ideas for organizing, financing, and mobilizing government undertakings are today, as then, marginalized by the factions that control the political process and the resources available to it. Only a small portion of the people the government serves are included in the constituency that actually selects the government.

Just as the transpartisan imperative enlivened the eighteenth century by fueling the creation of the American nation, it played a key nineteenth-century role in healing the nation from internal conflict, and it defended the nation from external attack in the twentieth. Now, at the dawn of the twenty-first century, it has yet another opportunity to add more to the America panorama. Twenty-first century American transpartisans, perhaps 130 million of them, have the opportunity to write the next chapter in the unfolding of democracy. In the words of American poet Walt Whitman:

> We have frequently printed the word Democracy. Yet I cannot too often repeat that it is a word the real gist of which still sleeps, quite unawaken'd, notwithstanding the resonance and the many angry tempests out of which its syllables have come, from pen or tongue. It is a great word, whose history, I suppose, remains unwritten, because that history has yet to be enacted. It is, in some sort, younger brother of another great and often-used word, Nature, whose history also waits unwritten.

Part IV

Transpartisan Politics: Bring Life Back to Society and Society Back to Life

Discussions of public policy tend to be limited to explorations of what policy *should be*, according to standards of fairness and efficiency. Mainstream policy analysts often overlook opportunities to include strategies on how their proposals could be achieved *politically*.

In our transpartisan view, we accept the challenge of presenting both our proposed solutions *and* our political strategies for mobilizing resources that will support our proposals. We make our substantive and procedural suggestions to start conversations. We hope these conversations will stimulate a large and growing audience concerned about these issues.

CHAPTER SEVEN

TRANSPARTISAN CAPITALISM II

It is commonly thought that capitalism has no place in solving certain major problems. Its critics think that market economics lacks the analytical tools, and its advocates believe markets are stymied by political interest groups that will never allow markets their proper role.

In this chapter we look at two major issues in which markets are commonly considered irrelevant: 1) the challenge of reforming public schools; and 2) the problems of energy and the environment. By looking through a transpartisan lens, one can find new possibilities for using markets to solve both of these problems.

Public Schools and the Challenge of Bureaucracy

Until his death in 2006, economist Milton Friedman was the world's leading proponent of free market capitalism. His idea of capitalism, however, was much broader than that held by many of either its proponents or its critics. While both capitalists and socialists regard the Israeli kibbutzim as socialist institutions because they are run communally without property rights, Friedman regarded them as a prime example of *capitalism* because they were chosen freely, without government compulsion. In Friedman's view, any institution is "capitalist" if people freely choose to be in it, even institutions commonly thought to be socialist. In his sense, therefore, it would be possible to say that communal organizations chosen freely are both "capitalist" and "socialist."[1]

Friedman's concept of capitalism is the market or freedom concept of capitalism, as we discussed in Chapter Three – as distinct from the business or order concept. Friedman's freedom concept is very different from the system critiqued by Marx, and it is also a much larger phenomenon than that embraced by most Western economists and supporters of capitalism. Our concept of capitalism goes even further. It includes Friedman's freedom of choice for *nongovernmental institutions*, and also applies it to the *government itself*.

Central to our idea of a transpartisan capitalism is the idea of *private property rights in both private and public space*. This is easy to see, for example, in the right of parents to be active "owners" of government schools. (The quotation marks are necessary because they are not, of course, owners in any legal sense, only in an informal, non-legal sense.) But in addition to parents, public schools need teachers, administrators, and bureaucrats to be stakeholders and to exercise responsibility as well as authority in making schools work. In successful, healthy schools, all are in fact "co-owners." In many others, especially in failing schools, there are no owners. Private rights in public space are essential, in fact, to making public institutions engaged, connected, and human places. They facilitate engaged, private experiences that are crucial to promote *public spirit*.

Again, we recall the experiment now unfolding in Washington, DC, with the public school system taking over formerly Catholic schools. If they carry over the sense of ownership that animated the old community and its schools, there is no reason why the new schools cannot succeed and, indeed, flourish. If they don't, the experiment will end tragically, and the schools will fail.

Ownership, in the sense we have been using it – not legal, but in spirit – is crucial to *caring*. It is an essential element to real engagement and commitment. It is made possible through the

authority of someone who has something valuable to give, participating in the school community and contributing to it. Bureaucrats can become "owners" (or capitalists in this sense) if they
are empowered to be free of the slavish allegiance to rules and
regulations and are given permission to exercise discretion in
working with the very people they are supposed to serve. They
can also become "owners" if they are motivated to help liberate
people in the schools to work together to make the schools work.

This does not mean there will be no rules or regulations.
All private and independent schools have rules that guide their
operation to be sure they remain true to their missions. These
school communities, however, have considerable authority and
latitude in establishing the school's mission and rules. We are
arguing that wide discretion should also be given to public
school bureaucrats and teachers to create similar guidelines.

Some may object that this *laissez faire* approach will, for
example, allow racists to organize schools that preach race hatred. This will not happen for two reasons. First, basic regulations
would forbid it, but a more basic reason is that the very nature
of what we are proposing — institutions that truly engage people — will encourage people to see past superficial differences
of class, race, religion, and so on, and see people as genuinely
"human." They will do this by institutionalizing communication
across loyalties and promoting trust among people who, in the
past, have had little contact and, thus, little trust. Racism happens when people don't engage, don't connect, and don't meet
each other as human beings. (The same is true for prejudice
related to gender, religion, and other qualities.) Although public schools should, today, promote such relationships, they often
do not. They institutionalize mechanical cultures with almost no
human contact, producing precisely the kind of environment that
feeds and sustains racism and other forms of prejudice.

The fear that trusting people will produce ugly results (*e.g.*, racist schools) is a classic artifact of an unengaged culture. It is the product of cultures in which people don't communicate across loyalties and so have no experience or trust in the magic that happens when people really engage one another.

Notes on a Political Strategy

No culture in modern societies is less engaged today than our political culture, which exists in a system that defines its *raison d'etre* in terms of non-engagement and active conflict. The political system is, thus sadly, the last place one can expect to find real leadership on these issues.

The reforms we are proposing for public schools would focus on empowering people at individual school sites – primarily teachers and administrators – to design reforms that would strengthen schools for the benefit of the particular student populations in them. For those who think this is radical, be reminded that charter and independent schools operate this way, as well as certain major public school districts.[2] We would also argue that the great majority of public schools that are actually working operate this way.[3]

A more important objection might arise if such decentralization takes place quickly, or all at once. After all, that is the normal way policy reforms are enacted: The legislature passes a law; or the executive issues an executive order; or the courts make a ruling compelling action; and everything changes on Tuesday.

We are not proposing that decentralization kick in all at once. It is not how people normally change. People change gradually, and that is how decentralization of authority in the schools should happen. A gradual process is important to allow timetables to be established that will work for people in different schools, and especially to prepare the schools – starting with the principals – for their new responsibilities.

Decentralizing authority is one way of increasing *choice* in public schools. Vouchers and charter schools — which are really vouchers given to communities rather than individuals — are more radical models for providing choice. The political impediments to choice can be considerable, especially regarding vouchers, as attempts to pass statewide voucher programs have failed dramatically.[4] Decentralizing authority can also be difficult politically, but the fact that it has been accomplished in various school districts at different times shows that it can be done. Moreover, unlike vouchers and charter schools, simple decentralization would not be exclusionary. Everyone would get to participate to the degree he or she wished.

In such a decentralized system, the responsibilities of the school district officials would shift from being mechanical traffic cops, directing traffic and giving people tickets, to being engaged and working to strengthen schools' capacities to succeed with increased authority. We are not sure how to do this, but we don't see why we should not give *bureaucrats* some choices on how to work with schools.

We explored in Chapter Two the pain that afflicts people who must work in mechanical, bureaucratic cultures. It is a struggle for them to avoid dying, and many surrender to the pressures. They are desperate for change, but their opposition to many proposals for reform suggests they can't tolerate it. This desperation for change yet resistance to it, we believe, may be found among bureaucrats and teachers alike. The resistance to change is commonly interpreted as being all about power: Once you have it, you don't want to share it. This is the common resistance factor found in both teachers' unions and bureaucracies.

A simple anecdote, drawn from real life, may reveal important things about individual teachers and how to make them feel they are valued, honored and appreciated — feelings that are all too rare in many parts of today's bureaucratic system. Let's return to the story of James Dierke, principal of the Visitacion Valley Middle School in San Francisco, which we told in Chapter Two. Dierke, if you remember, took over the leadership of an inner-city school in the most dangerous neighborhood in the city, with all of the major signs of dysfunction that are common to such schools. Because careers in school administration are often not well served by posts such as Visitacion Valley, the school district had trouble finding someone willing to be its principal. Dierke was informed of his appointment the day before fall term was to begin. When he arrived, he found a demoralized staff who received few benefits for what was clearly very hard duty. Dierke relays a conversation he had with one teacher that highlights both the trouble and the opportunity at schools like this.

"I wanted to talk to him about [the proposed reform], which I wanted to introduce," Dierke recalled.

"Oh, that will never work here; there will be no support for it," was the depressed, knee-jerk response from the teacher.

"Well, I want to do it anyway. The trouble is, I don't know *how* to do it, and I need your help. I would like you to take a few days off and design it for me. Recruit one or two others to help you, and then please bring me your recommendations in, let's say, ten days. Oh, and by the way, I plan to allocate $1,000 of the school's discretionary budget to implement the reform."

The teacher came back on fire with enthusiasm for the ideas he had developed. Why the change of heart? Because someone actually cared what he thought, gave him time off to work on his recommendations, was committed to implement them, and had actually allocated real money to make sure it worked.

It is a simple little story that highlights both the problem and the solution. Most people don't like being dead; they want to be alive. Give them the smallest chance for life, and they will grab it.

Teachers' unions often seem to oppose any attempt at reform. These unions end up supporting the status quo and opposing change — no matter how ugly the status quo — and there is no single model they support. They support the decentralized models in Edmonton, Canada, in Seattle, in Houston, and in New York City, District Two. They support the highly centralized systems in most other places. The degree of centralization obviously affects their power; yet they support all levels of centralization. William Ouchi, author of *Making Schools Work*, argues that the more centralized a school district's spending, the less it spends on teaching. Districts like Edmonton, Canada, which decentralize most of their funding to individual schools, spend far more of their budgets on teaching (fifty-seven percent) than highly centralized districts like Los Angeles, which spend much less (thirty-three percent). The union's power would obviously be best served by decentralization, which results in more spending on teaching; yet they continue to support the status quo.

The fact that decentralization has been accomplished in successful schools more than once and in different states shows that it will not meet anywhere near the same resistance that confronts voucher proposals and, to some degree, charter schools. What is crucial to make decentralization work is gradual change and consistent, sustained technical assistance to individual schools in order to build the capacity to make it work.

The Energy/Environment Challenge

A host of issues arise in the current debate on global warming as a possibly life-threatening issue facing the planet. These are the most difficult and politically troublesome issues we face. Both sides warn of doom if the other side wins. On one side, environmentalists warn about the end of the planet caused by global warming, and on the other, their opponents warn about hugely negative impacts on the global economy, especially on the poorest countries, of doing what the environmentalists say is necessary. Energy and the environment are inextricably connected: one (energy) controlled by the left, because the left's support is needed to accomplish political action supporting energy production; and the other (the environment) by the right, because the right's support is key to accomplishing major political action supporting the environment.

The intellectual issue is further complicated by a *political* debate that pretends to track the intellectual debate but in reality is largely disconnected from it. In fact, it is hard to avoid making the following point in brutally direct terms: Liberals in the political debate *pretend* they follow the environmentalist position on climate change, and neither the media nor conservatives "blow the whistle" on them. Liberal politicians incant environmentalist concerns about climate change and support *symbolic* actions that embrace the environmentalist position. But when it comes to doing anything serious — for example, cutting carbon emissions — they are MIA. Democrats controlled Congress for years up until 1994, and again from 2006 to 2008, and took no serious environmental action.

One simple proposal for cutting carbon emissions while also reducing the enormous wealth transfers to Middle East oil producers would be to impose a tax on carbon-based fuel for automobiles, planes, and so forth. Various economists have proposed this, including "free market" economists such as Harvard economist and Bush advisor Gregory Mankiw. Such a tax would increase the cost of using carbon-based fuel and would, therefore, reduce its use over time. Because demand takes time to change, the tax could start low and increase over time so people would factor in future fuel costs when they buy their next car. A tax on carbon-based fuel would also increase the use of alternative fuels, which may become less expensive. This would further reduce the enormous outflow of money going to Middle East countries — some of it, ultimately, to terrorists.

The arguments for such a tax are strong. Nevertheless, political support is hard to find for it, whether Congress is controlled by Democrats or Republicans. While president, Bill Clinton tried to get a tax through Congress, but Congress was willing to support only a trivial tax. Al Gore, who was vice president then, is now the principal global advocate of serious action on the issue. But serious political support for a tax is simply not there. According to the paradoxical logic of major political changes (see Chapter Eleven), a serious proposal for action on climate change must come from Republicans and conservatives, whose support is necessary to unite the political culture for the issue; it cannot come from Democrats. This is obvious from the lack of interest in serious tax proposals in Democratic primary rhetoric in the 2008 election; if and when Democrats retake the White House, it will, unfortunately, be further characterized by a lack of action. Accomplishing serious action on carbon emissions will depend on engaging the transpartisan majority.

We think such a tax makes sense. It makes sense on a scale that is not, at present, politically feasible. From a transpartisan perspective, we think it is not useful to spend time here trying to restate the substantive issues. We prefer, rather, to shift and focus only on possible *political* solutions. We do this because, unless proposals for solutions have a chance to play politically, they are irrelevant. That is where most proposals are today, which explains why they are going nowhere.

What is Politically Feasible?

Two lines of thought suggest themselves here, one involving substance and the other involving *process*. The substantive line of thought involves possible approaches that might stimulate broad political support. We see three approaches here (though we are sure there are more):

Reduce subsidies to energy producers;

Reform the metrics used to measure the environmental impacts of energy use; and

Expand emissions trading, already widely in use.

The instrumental line of thought focuses on the process by which political leaders will decide what to do — or, put another way — this approach asks *whose arguments* will ultimately win out in the debate?

At a meeting sponsored in June 2006 by Reuniting America on energy and the environment, there was wide support among both conservatives and liberals for reducing subsidies to various industries to promote different kinds of energy. Such subsidies were seen ultimately as subsidies to energy consumption. Of course, both the "energy side" (conservatives) and "environment side" (liberals) had their own favored energy producers. (The quotation marks are necessary because these are crude generalizations of positions that were in fact much more complicated.)

Most people agreed it was best to give up all the subsidies — including those targeted on alternative energies — but based on the experience of the Energy Policy Act of 2005, both sides came to the conclusion that in the real world Congress could not resist awarding subsidizes in response to the requests of political interest groups.

At the meeting, there was also widespread unhappiness expressed about the metrics used to measure the environmental impacts of energy use. This is potentially a very large subject, which will create opportunities for input from a wide variety of experts, including natural scientists and economists.

It is also already obvious that emissions trading stimulates strong interest and support across the political spectrum, which explains why it is already in broad use. Emissions trading is valuable *both on its own terms and as a model for policy formation in related areas.* According to Alan P. Loeb, former senior attorney in the Office of Air and Radiation at the U.S. Environmental Protection Agency, experiences in both lead phase-down and acid rain show that emissions trading is significantly efficient to satisfy businesses, environmentalists, and a wide array of other interests. In order for trading to *exist*, Loeb says, "it must first *come into* existence," but a consensus must be formed before a market can be adopted, which begs questions of equity among the participants to the negotiations. When emissions trading is introduced for consideration in the design of a regulatory program, the anticipated efficiency it will generate creates a "zone of possible agreement" which competing interests can share, and all become better off if the process is successful. Industry can obtain cost reductions, and environmental groups can obtain more stringent emission standards as well as assurance that these standards will be achieved. The possibility of all parties winning helps promote agreement.

The key is to unlock the long-standing "zero-sum" game. By advancing the interests of both industry and environmental groups, trading makes consensus possible. The implications are far-reaching. Experience tells us that trading, if properly implemented, can transform the structure, incentives, regulatory politics, and public acceptability of traditional command-and-control rules. It is important to note, however, that the environmental benefits tend to occur in the design of the program, while the economic benefits occur in the individual trades.

Stated in historical terms, emissions trading makes it possible to restore a harmonious order that contains both firm, unambiguous codes of responsibility yet procedural flexibility. Experience makes it clear that the confrontational approach to regulation is unnecessary when industry abandons its assertion that it has the right to pollute and accepts the legitimacy of regulation. Settling that core issue restores a sense of trust and opens up the possibility that environmental groups and regulators will accept more cost-effective instruments to achieve their regulatory goals.

The emissions trading approach as presented by Loeb is a virtual textbook case of transpartisan procedures. Trust, responsibility, flexibility, obtaining a zone of agreement, and initiating a connected, trusting relationship among affected parties, without a set notion of outcomes, all create an opportunity to actually solve a real problem.

Who Will Decide What to Do on Climate Change?

It is hard to exaggerate the intensity of the debate on climate change and the fear it generates on both sides. Both sides believe the other side is advocating no less than a catastrophe. How do we adjudicate the conflict?

One way is to ask what arguments could persuade political leaders to act decisively, one way or the other? (The operative word in that sentence is "could"; such arguments would not *guarantee* success, but there would be *no chance* of success without them.) In any debate on climate change, *economic arguments* will ultimately play the greatest role in determining what is done. This will be true in both Democratic and Republican administrations. Economists will have most to say because their perspective encompasses the broadest field of issues and arguments — the broad field of the costs and benefits of all possible actions, including all those argued by natural scientists.

We are not scientists, and we will express no opinions about the scientific arguments. We do believe that disagreements among scientists have been largely unreported in the media, and this is unfortunate. We *are* certain that the key group that needs to be persuaded is the *economists*. And up to now, neither the economists who normally advise Republican administrations nor those who advise Democratic administrations have been persuaded.

We have noted earlier, however, that some important economists on both sides have been persuaded that climate change is a real problem and that a tax on carbon-based energy would start to reduce carbon-based fuel use, pending more scientific evidence. (And, as we have noted, the case for such a tax would also serve important national security objectives.)

Although we have said we think Republicans and conservatives are key to taking significant action on climate change (because they hold the key to uniting the political culture for action on this issue), the magnitude of the challenge of getting political support for the crash program desired by many environmentalists can be understood by asking: Who could persuade a Democratic administration to take serious action? Again, it will be economists, doing cost-benefit analysis to ensure that the costs of actions proposed do not exceed the benefits. Economists are often difficult to persuade, as indicated by the distinguished economists who participated in the Copenhagen Consensus (including four Nobel Prize winners), who were skeptical about the need for a crash program that would impose substantial costs on economies everywhere.[5]

We take no position on the debate. Some of the issues are extremely technical, especially the issue of the "discount rate" used to estimate the current value of a future event with a very low probability, for instance, catastrophic climate change. Other issues and trade-offs, which rarely make it into the public debate, also need to be considered: Besides the huge (half-trillion-dollar) wealth transfer for imported oil to unsavory people (including terrorists), the biofuel alternative is creating competition between food and fuel, thus increasing the cost of food for the world's poor.

Finally (again relating to political feasibility), there is the challenge of getting Congressional action that is not ninety percent motivated by narrow political interests. An example, at the present time, is the government's current subsidies for production of high-cost domestic ethanol, which benefit U.S. farmers with almost no net gain for the environment (because it costs almost as much energy to produce the ethanol as the value of the energy output). At the same time – again, pitched to the farm vote – we forbid imports of low cost ethanol from Brazil. The transpartisan challenge, of course, is to produce support for policies actually aimed at energy and environmental objectives rather than at political interest groups.

Many economists, including those who advise Democratic administrations, believe the costs of a crisis program enacted immediately would far exceed the benefits, and that we need to work on a variety of fronts to solve the problem over a longer time period.

*   *   *

We have focused here on how "capitalism," or economic markets, may be used to solve two major issues: the challenge of public school reform and the hugely troublesome issues of energy and the environment. In reviewing how these issues are currently being debated, we believe, reluctantly, that the principal terms in the debate, including the word "capitalism" itself, have been so distorted and so charged with ideological baggage, that they may be all but useless for the task of creating transpartisan solutions to these problems.

Solving the problem of public schools requires importing the spirit of ownership into the public system by all of the principal stakeholders in public schools: parents, teachers, children, administrators, and bureaucrats. Solving the huge challenges of energy and the environment will depend on persuading economists that the costs of proposed reforms do not exceed their benefits. Since economists of all stripes, Democrats and Republicans alike, are students of market economics, market analyses will provide the solution for these issues.

The failure of engaged and collaborative political behavior reduces most of the major actors on all of these issues to simplistic visions of darkness and light that conceal major opportunities to solve problems currently entombed in political stalemates. Thinking with a transpartisan openness to expand political coalitions may reveal new opportunities for political breakthroughs that are now entirely hidden. We hope the discussion above suggests how to bring government bureaucrats and teachers' unions into active support of public school reform. We also hope our readers now see possibilities for bringing national security experts into the debate on global warming and also for deploying arguments about insurance as support for implementing a tax on carbon-based fuels. We do not know the outcome of these various conversations but we know they must take place.

The broader lesson here is to broaden the debate and stop the narrow, moralistic condemnations that are shutting down possibilities for reform. These are important issues in desperate need of solution. It is hard to imagine how they will go anywhere until we start talking to each other in new ways.

CHAPTER EIGHT

RECRUITING CITIZENS AS PARTNERS FOR NATIONAL SECURITY AND FOREIGN POLICY

In the past 75 years, Nazi Germany, the Soviet Union, Communist China and their satellite states were all considered threats to the U.S., and U.S. foreign policy was designed to deal with these nation states. Since 9/11, it has become clear that governments are no longer the principal threats to security; nonstate actors and culture have become the principal challenges.

It is widely believed that American foreign policy is in crisis. Critics of President George W. Bush believe he is the problem and that a change of leadership will put everything right. They are wrong. The debate on foreign policy is all about pretending that weak states are strong and are able to promote economic and political reforms. The foreign policy community appears neither capable of understanding and engaging the nonstate sector nor influencing weak states to make them more effective.

The preoccupation with states ignores the lessons of periods in history when nonstate actors dominated states and empires. In his new book, *Fighting Identity*, Michael Vlahos argues that a burgeoning nonstate sector was a major factor in transforming the Roman Empire in late antiquity and was also powerful at the end of the Middle Ages in weakening the Byzantine Empire and opening the way for the Ottoman world. Vlahos argues that we are now losing wars because we are choosing to fight our enemies not on our terms but on terms defined by passionate communities whose compelling visions are both validated by our losses and, ironically, legitimated through our victories. The result is that we are empowering nonstate groups at our expense. Those we have made our enemies are trading on powerful, emerging identities of peoples animated by the desire for independence, while using our network technology, like cell phones and the Internet, to realize their aims. New identities and alternative communities are following a path that we once sought more than two centuries ago. We have become the system-leader fighting to hold on to the world that once reified us, so much so that we are literally fighting a change we do not like — we are fighting identity. The paradox is simple: the more we struggle against the demand for new identity, the more we accelerate the erosion of our system. We essentially become the symbiotic helpers of what we fear: the midwife of a new future.

These circumstances offer us opportunities that our current polices, driven by fear and short on trust, deny. The Bush administration made a major mistake in thinking that the people of Iraq would embrace us as their liberators and usher in a smooth transition to democracy. It assumed that their appetite for democracy could overcome their historic loyalties to tribe and religion, which has often led to internal conflict. (This was, in fact, an important difference between our historical experience and theirs.) It failed to appreciate the importance of *social trust* to democracy, because without trust there could be no commitment to protect minority rights — an essential component without which democratic systems cannot work. The situation in Iraq, whether going well or going badly at any particular moment, makes this point each day. Without social trust democracy fails.

We have said that engaging local civil society is the key to promoting economic, political, and even cultural change. Governments — both our government and the weak governments in countries like Iraq — cannot accomplish these changes because they operate mechanically, by commands, and changes in societies need to happen organically, by persuasion.

A key principle in promoting change is *local ownership*. The possibilities for change are greatly enhanced when local institutions take the lead in proposing and promoting it. On the other hand, when the U.S. Government appropriates $75 million to promote democracy in Iran, it contaminates everything financed by the money. Funding needs to be made by independent bodies such as the National Endowment for Democracy (NED).

Working with civil society will ensure that local ownership exists. There are powerful models for working with civil society organizations in promoting economic development, educating girls and empowering women, recruiting citizens as partners for promoting democracy and peace, and a variety of activities in societies that occur before and after conflicts.[1]

While these models exist, the government at this time has, unfortunately, little or no capacity to either identify or invest in them at strategic scales.[2]

Focusing on Social Trust

Trust is a crucial issue that needs to be addressed, especially in relation to the Arab and Muslim countries that have become the new priorities for foreign and national security policy. Trust is essential for both peace and democracy. It is also essential for market economies and economic development.

Powerful examples of civil society initiatives promoting social trust in places with extreme conflict, including religious conflict, do exist. Two of the most important examples are Northern Ireland and South Africa.

Brandeis political scientist Mari Fitzduff has studied civic engagement and the trust it enabled in Northern Ireland, which led to the 1998 signing of a reasonably stable peace between Catholics and Protestants. Hundreds of informal mediation initiatives and dialogues sponsored by community mediators, academics, churches, business, trade unions, and perhaps most importantly, women, supported the formal negotiations. These initiatives focused on facilitating communications between disputants and politicians, paramilitaries and governments, and politicians and civil society. Other initiatives aimed at stimulating dialogue through media, drama, music, and art programs. These initiatives generally avoided issues related to the conflict, leaving those to the formal negotiations. Focusing instead on the economy, jobs, and social issues, the central purpose of these initiatives was to build trust and eventually a culture of peace, making it safe for politicians to consider issues of common interest.

In South Africa between 1991 and 1994, when the first elections were held, initiatives by nonstate actors such as religious groups, civil society organizations (CSOs),[3] businesses, and trade unions promoted communication and dialogue all over the country, and helped South Africa avoid the bloodbath that many had predicted there. In addition, once the new society emerged, South Africa pioneered the Peace and Reconciliation Commission process in which punishment was waived for individuals who came forward with information that acknowledged their previous crimes and helped create a common, accepted history, which was one essential component to developing community trust. This process has spread around the world and is currently one of the most useful undertakings for examining transpartisan processes at work such as the work done by the Amy Biehl Foundation.[4]

There has been no peace and so little democracy in the Middle East because of low levels of social trust and very limited commitment to any civic engagement aimed at promoting that trust. (Dennis Ross, President Carter's negotiator for the Middle East, now acknowledges this was the great missing piece in the peace process during the Clinton years.) Current policies in the Middle East are failing in their efforts to promote democracy. Civil society initiatives are also the only source of hope for lasting peace in such troubled states as Indonesia, Egypt, and Somalia.

Designing foreign policies for societies in weak states will be difficult because our foreign policymakers have almost no theory or experiences to guide them. Much of the debate on the weak states that have become the new threats to our security is decidedly fatalistic. This fatalism will continue until policymakers develop new, society-based instruments designed to address deeper social and cultural issues, and position them to support the traditional instruments of foreign policy.

The new, emerging transpartisan community needs to embrace the development of social and cultural organizations and create both the theory and practical models that will make it an increasingly important instrument in foreign policy.

A Foreign Policy Model

To accomplish the objectives we have sketched here will require a substantial investment of public funds, and since the independence of both the funding agency and local civil society organizations is crucial to the integrity of this model, it cannot work unless people trust each other at each stage of the process. This means that government, senior policy-makers, and Congress must trust the funding agency, and the funding agency must trust its grantees.

We propose a process that does two paradoxical things: first, it designs and funds civil society initiatives to achieve particular foreign policy objectives; and second, it works informally, without apparent connections to policy.

How can such a system which operates according to two, apparently opposite, principles work? The reason government policymakers struggle to understand this system, is that they are accustomed to operating only through formal mechanisms — by commands. For example, the Bush administration decided it wanted foreign aid to operate more directly with foreign policy so the Secretary of State announced a major reorganization: the administrator of USAID would go to the State Department and assume the new title of director of foreign assistance. Then this person would also be the director of USAID. This formal structure converted the whole of the U.S. foreign assistance program into a U.S. foreign policy program. Or, to put the point more precisely, it creates the *perception* that it is now officially a program of U.S. foreign policy. For many people in other countries, this contaminates the entire program, and it also contaminates the institutions that take the money, reducing their authority and effectiveness, which are so necessary to the perceptions of their independence.

There is another way to accomplish the same objective, but without the huge cost of reduced effectiveness. This alternative is easy for people to understand in their private lives, even if they may struggle to understand it in the world of formal, institutional authority. The alternate model is to operate *informally*, without commands, allowing both the funder and ultimate recipients to exercise their own judgment, while informally advising them on both broad strategic objectives and specific programs.

How do officials ensure the cooperation of the funder and its grantees? The system would operate informally but with substantial cooperation ensured by annual refunding reviews; if either party balks at how the relationship is working, the relationship ends.

If real trust animates the process, this informal system of consultation and collaboration should operate in both directions. Policymakers at the top, who are responsible for funding, should form their plans in active cooperation and consultation both with the funder and also with people closest to the ground — the civil society organizations that will do the work.

In considering the challenge of social trust, it is possible that this may turn out to be as problematic in the United States as it is in the Arab and Muslim countries. Unfortunately, the enormous conflict tearing apart our political system is mired in massive distrust: major political parties toward each other, policymakers toward the bureaucrats who must implement the policies, and citizens toward their government.

Spending for Security

There is broad agreement that at the present time the United States is expected to be the guarantor of the world order. However, one of the greatest challenges to U.S. policy is to take responsibility for that leadership role in a way that still leaves space for other countries to contribute in meaningful ways. Without that space, the U.S. will be forced to assume far too much of the burden in the face of huge, forthcoming constraints in other areas of its budget. After the Iraq experience, it is unlikely that the U.S. will have an appetite for any military adventures in the near future.

Since 9/11, spending for defense has increased substantially. Today it amounts to about $500 billion per year in the base budget — as much as the spending of countries with the sixteen next largest economies in the world, combined. Counting the add-ons for Iraq and Afghanistan, the U.S. spends as much as the next fifty-two countries, forty-two of which are U.S. allies.

While we are spending $500 billion on military programs aimed at protecting national security, we are only spending $20 billion on nonmilitary, foreign assistance programs. However, our security problem is not ninety-five percent military and less than five percent non-military; this creates a serious imbalance between where we actually spend our money and where we need to, in our opinion. Although we do not recommend any wholesale money transfers from military to foreign assistance in its current form, we are inclined to recommend reducing defense spending and undertaking a serious review of foreign assistance programs to increase their strategic impact. However, serious transpartisan consideration of this possibility in safe public spaces built on social trust can determine if such a recommendation is sound. Only after such a serious review would we then recommend substantially increasing spending for strategic, non-military programs.

Encouraging other countries to increase their sharing of the burden of global military responsibilities will require sharing responsibility for designing and implementing policies with them. Informal consultation on different activities and issues and in different theaters centered on strategically important objectives could create real ownership opportunities, even by small countries. This could mitigate the United States' overwhelming hegemonic role in the world, a role that leaves no significant place for any other countries. Not being given a meaningful role only breeds resentment and often produces passive resistance.

This will be another occasion to apply the principle of *local ownership* by letting other countries "own" various pieces of strategies developed consensually. This should add incentives to increase their investments and reduce our burden. And if policymakers will commit to a strategy that includes serious investment in civil society initiatives, they will find that military force will recede as a strategic priority. As in our discussion of the paradoxical logic of policy reform (Chapter Eleven), this is transpartisan because it depends on the U.S. withdrawing from some international theaters and empowering other countries to play increased roles there.

CHAPTER NINE

RE-ENGAGING SOCIETY:
RACE, GAYS, RELIGION, AND SPIRITUALITY

When political action on behalf of "underdog groups" was an active part of the political debate, advocacy focused on legal rights, which were established by courts and implemented by force. Public, legal acceptance was important, but it was obviously not enough. Many groups, especially African-Americans and gays, continue to feel like victims or under-classes in America.

As civil rights laws reduced and eliminated public discrimination, private discrimination became more wounding and more difficult to address. "Political correctness," for a time, tried to address the problem by introducing euphemisms that denied obvious realities (i.e., that short people were, in fact, short; and that the handicapped were, in fact, handicapped). But people resented heavy-handed attempts to tell them what to say and eventually came to understand that pretending things are true that obviously are not is alienating. Political correctness made private acceptance and connection virtually impossible.

Believing that real reconciliation and acceptance between people can occur through public action alone (without private engagement and connection) is a tragic mistake. It exhibits a grotesquely shallow misunderstanding of where the deepest levels of human interaction take place. Truly personal engagements allow people to value and honor each other — not in spite of their differences, but in open acceptance and respect of them.

This happens in relationships where, implicitly, people say, "Our differences of race, class, and religion are less significant than the fact that we are both human beings. Our *humanness* is the point of connection where we can be truly equal. And that is the point where we can realize some of our highest aspirations and possibilities as human beings."

The greatest opportunities for transpartisan collaboration lie in spaces where empowered private citizens can share public responsibilities and contribute to solving major issues — sometimes decisively. Individual familiarity and parity enables public policy to move away from its traditional, mechanistic functions toward a more organic, engaged, consensual process. Rather than fomenting opposition, public policy can often suppress it by being transpartisan.

We believe that responsibilities freely chosen and accepted are more likely to be honored than responsibilities that are imposed. We also believe that *objective* resolutions of public problems are more likely to be achieved when they are the outcome of active, *subjective* personal connections and experience.

The keys to *private* acceptance and respect are personal engagement and connection. These should be the foundation of sound and effective *public* engagement and policy, as well. The principal impediments to such engagements today are external, rule-driven moral systems, whether emanating from traditional institutions (capitalist or religious), progressive institutions (socialist or union), or political correctness. What we believe is broken and how we can fix it will be obvious from our discussions of race, gender and sexual preference, and religion, and applies to any group that perceives itself as "excluded" or "disadvantaged."

Race

Although the civil rights laws have accomplished important reforms in race relations in the U.S., it is clear from the continuing struggles of African-Americans that race remains a serious concern in twenty-first century America. Except perhaps in entertainment and sports, many black Americans continue to feel treated like second-class citizens honored largely in destructive, nihilistic forms celebrated most notably by the dark side of the rapper culture. The real issue here has to do with relationships between individual people. The real challenge is to develop a combination of institutions, leadership, and citizen action that will promote real engagement between and among individual people.

The idea that solutions to the race problem rest with one side of the political spectrum or the other (left or right) is itself an artifact of the mechanistic idiom that shapes all public policy-making, not only in the United States but in virtually every country. It is an idiom that is all about governments, and it brings with it a weak concept of citizenship. In fact, it leaves almost no room for citizens at all. Yet the problem of race – like many other problems, we believe – is now largely about how citizens engage, or fail to engage, each other. It is about how people treat each other. It is subjective.

The challenge of engaging people so they see each other as human beings rather than as blacks or gays or Muslims or Christians or Jews is the same challenge as engaging people to reform public schools, promote health, and address the foreign policy challenge of promoting social trust in weak states. In the United States, nothing could improve race relations more than engaging people and empowering them to play meaningful roles in reforming the schools. This is especially important, to the extent that bussing is going to continue, so that we can at least discard the practice of forcing people far from their homes into newly segregated environments (the internally segregated schools).

The victim identity (see Chapter Five) has a powerful and unfortunate effect on how African-Americans perceive the *possibility* of progress. For any group to progress, it must believe it is *possible* to progress. The victim identity, however, tends to encourage well-meaning people to regard claims of black success as a kind of conceptual mistake; African-Americans claiming to be successful are often attacked as being untrue to their authentic communities. To the extent that African-Americans believe this, the victim identity systematically undermines the possibility of their, our, and the rest of society's success in transcending racial barriers.

Leadership is another issue that needs to be mentioned in regard to African-Americans. All communities, to progress, need strong leaders. Lawyers play an important role in political communities. In the case of African-Americans, government policies are inflicting great harm on black lawyers, thus undermining the community's leadership class.

The problem arises in government programs that finance lawyers for the poor. The common practice is for the government to subsidize lawyers to serve poor clients. In many places, this means encouraging white, middle-class poverty lawyers to take clients away from the indigenous black lawyers who must charge for their services. A major effect of the program is to pay these poverty lawyers to take clients away from the indigenous black bar, thus harming the black leadership class. If we are to promote strong leadership, why not subsidize clients rather than lawyers, and let the clients choose whom they want to pay to represent them? Not having to compete with the "free" legal services provided by the government would strengthen the financial foundation of black leaders and would strengthen the bonds between the black community and its leaders.

Gender and Sexual Preference

Gays commonly fear revealing their "secret" to straight people. They only feel comfortable in doing so when they are engaged and connected with "straights" who accept them as they accept themselves. However, we must acknowledge that the subjective side of this issue is more difficult to solve for gays than for blacks. The most powerful way beliefs on this issue are changed occurs when someone has a child who is gay. It changes the family forever, because family relationships are the most engaged and connected relationships most people ever experience.

We have one, major proposal here, which has powerful relevance to many of the arguments we have made in this essay. We are choosing to mention it here because it may have the largest effect on this issue.

Public policy is typically about *objective* issues relating to masses of people. Thus, our public leaders spend all of their time providing "leadership" by tending to stay in capital cities or traveling in a security bubble, making speeches, promoting policy reforms, signing bills, and participating in the rest of the trappings of the "political" life. The challenge of "gay rights" is an extremely private, *subjective* challenge. As such, the venue in which it is played out is as far removed from the public life of our political leaders as anything could be.

Our political leaders do not, at present, see it as part of their job to shine lights on private behavior, yet our entire trans-partisan message has to do with recruiting citizens as partners to accomplish public ends. Our political leaders play on stages, which, when lit up by the media, can serve powerful educational purposes. Arnold Schwarzenegger in California is the most obvious example. If Governor Schwarzenegger were to devote two days a month to traveling around California, visiting citizens reaching out to each other in ways that promote public ends — blacks and whites working together in schools, gays and straights working together in inner-city youth programs for disadvantaged youth — the possibilities would be endless. The media would follow him everywhere and reveal to everyone the intimacy and power of personal engagement that is at the heart of purpose and meaning in life. It's what people live for.

Religion and Spirituality

At one time, it seemed that religion was declining as an issue in the United States as well as other developed countries. Today, however, it seems to be growing, as religion becomes more involved in domestic politics and as it has become perhaps the major stimulant to international violence. The American commitment to separation of church and state makes it hard for the United States government to be involved with religion. This poses a serious problem for U.S. foreign policy, because religion may now be the greatest issue we face both for foreign policy and national security.

Conflict among religions is a problem only when religion becomes objectified. There is no problem when the focus is on *spirit*, because spirit transcends particular practices and beliefs – the things that people fight about. The importance of religion as a source of aggression may best be understood by considering the results of a study of all reported incidents of conflict between Hindus and Muslims in India between 1950 and 1995. In his book *Ethnic Conflict and Civic Life*, Ashutosh Varshney explains why some communities were able to maintain relative peace while others exploded into ghastly violence:

> The pre-existing local networks of civic engagement between the two communities [Hindu and Muslim] stand out as the single most important *proximate* causes. Where such networks of engagement exist, tensions and conflict were regulated and managed; where they are missing, communal identities led to endemic and ghastly violence.'

The essential variable is not the intensity of religious belief; it is those networks of engagement connecting people, stimulating trust, and facilitating cooperation to contain and limit violence. "Religious rage," which is commonly blamed for violence in these countries, appears where networks of civic engagement connecting people are missing.

The solution to this issue of warring religions may be found in accepting that the essence of religion is really spirit. When religious beliefs, rituals, and sacred texts are in a state of connection – connection to self, to others, to Nature, to the Cosmos, and to God – they are true to the highest calling of religion, to its essential spirit. In this perspective, rituals and beliefs of particular religions are the means to the end of connection through spirit. When religious rituals become the ends, a condition which characterizes "holy wars," the connection to spirit is weakened and then lost. History attests to the unspeakable brutality that can result when that connection is lost. Because religious vision depicts the highest sense of human possibility, it can lead either to the ultimate sense of religious aspiration or, when objectified, to the lowest depths of human brutality.

Because we commonly separate understanding of religious and spiritual life from the rest of life, we also commonly misperceive how commitment to spirit is at the very heart of solutions to every public policy challenge that depends on human engagement. Commitment to the spirit of connection, in fact, is an essential component for solving every policy challenge that now seems beyond reach – from race to poverty to international conflict.

The rigorous determination to separate spiritual understanding from routine life comes from a centuries-old intellectual tradition that tends to identify spirit with church and confine it to organized religion. This habit so dominates the Western intellectual idiom that we are blocked from seeing how it has contributed to the nightmare mechanistic world we inhabit and that is especially, and tragically obvious in public spaces, like schools and bureaucracies, and in our foreign policy.

We know spirit in private but tend to deny it in public. We deny it, particularly in its political manifestation, in the mechanistic terms of our intellectual idiom. Awakening our innate potential requires empowering spirit in all of its diverse manifestations. Amy Sullivan, a self-identified evangelical liberal Democrat, wrote one of the articles under the headline "Evangelical Liberals? More of us than you think." In a companion article "It's Not Your Father's Religious Right," David Kuo, former deputy director of the White House Office on Faith-Based and Community Initiatives, reported that:

> a late July online poll of 1,000 evangelicals from Beliefnet.
> com found that [while] ... seventy percent still said that ending abortion was important or very important; [and] almost fifty percent opposed same-sex marriage... sixty percent identified themselves as part of a political movement interested more in 'protecting the environment, tackling HIV/AIDS, alleviating poverty and promoting human rights and less on abortion and homosexuality.' Among the issues most concerning them were reducing poverty, improving health care and education, and stopping torture.

Sullivan addressed abortion in her article, reporting that "in the fall of 2006, two Catholic Democrats in the House of Representatives, the anti-abortion Tim Ryan and the pro-abortion rights Rosa DeLauro, introduced legislation to reduce abortion rates by preventing unwanted pregnancies and providing support to pregnant women and new parents. That same fall, an anti-abortion Catholic Democrat, Bill Ritter, won the Colorado governorship after convincing his party's activists and donors that a pro-life politician need not be actively anti-choice. In a few states, pro-choice Democratic candidates sat down with evangelical and Catholic leaders to talk about abortion. They didn't back down from defending women's right to choose, but they won with support levels from Catholics and evangelicals that were ten to fifteen points above the party's national average in the midterm elections."

A landmark study of religion in America, the U.S. Religious Landscape Survey provided important information on the context of the shifting political nature of American religion.[2] Based on interviews with more than 35,000 Americans age eighteen and older, the study found that religion in the U.S. is increasingly diverse and fluid — "a vibrant marketplace where individuals pick and choose religions that meet their needs," leaving religious groups to compete for members. The study found that nearly half of American adults say they have left the faith tradition of their upbringing, either by switching to a different religious group or choosing not to affiliate with a faith tradition at all.[3]

We believe the contrast between the reality of American religion as fluid, and the harsh religious certitudes that have characterized some recent political campaigns, further illustrates the tension between mechanistic and organic public expression.

Debating the right to abortion, whatever the merits, is mechanical. Working to reduce the number of abortions is organic. When the transpartisan space opens, the organic essence can be seen. For example, there is broad social consensus that the fewer abortions the better. There is no credible "pro increasing abortion" constituency. This creates an opportunity for the members of society to work together to reduce abortions, including the twenty-five to fifty percent of all pregnancies that end in spontaneous abortions. Like all the other issues we describe, shifting the abortion question from mechanistic partisan debates to organic problem-solving creates an opportunity for individuals of diverse political orientations to work together to solve an important social problem.

Members of a society of connected individuals resist demonizing each other and embrace working together to solve real problems. Nurturing the spirit of religion as part of this whole effort gives strength that the mechanical focus undermines. Issues of race, gender, and religion — among the most intractable in our partisan political culture — seem much more addressable when considered in a connected organic community. Such issues lend themselves to transpartisan treatment. They are places where the transpartisan imperative offers opportunity and hope.

Part V

Leadership for a New American Politics

The discussion to this point has been focused on particular issues. In this section we turn to practical issues of how to organize
citizen initiatives for change, how to approach the challenges of
promoting large policy change using "paradoxical" logic, and
some large issues that are not currently visible in the political
debate, but perhaps should be.

CHAPTER TEN

TRANSPARTISAN: PAST, PRESENT, AND FUTURE

American politics today is a narrow, brittle structure, featuring stylized debates that only marginally relate to actual political beliefs. The mass media reinforce the problem, magnifying conflict while marginalizing cooperation. The whole enterprise makes a strong country of widely shared values, unique common experiences, and collective expectations appear confused, conflicted, contentious, and weak.

Walking is our principal metaphor. It makes little sense to debate whether to walk on just the left leg or the right leg. In political debate, it makes no more sense to argue that only "left" solutions or only "right" solutions work best, because these strong political positions present only partial views of reality. It doesn't take much reflection to realize that the society we actually want to live in will feature important values from the *left*, the *right*, and from the *freedom* and *order* positions of both. Nevertheless, our political leaders continue to insist that their views are the only correct ones in their appeals to an increasingly disenchanted public. Just as people naturally walk on both legs — not just the left or right — they also naturally stray from strictly partisan positions.

The artificial terms of debate result from several factors, both political and philosophical. Paramount among these are:

> Our preoccupying focus on the government as the only source of "public" action,

Our ignorance of how citizens need to participate in effective public activities – both in nonstate action and even in the government itself, and

The influence of the mass media, especially television, which view fighting over government largesse as the most riveting theatrical material available for the evening news.

Limiting our politics to static liberal/conservative clichés makes no more sense than clapping with one hand; it handicaps us. Labels like "most liberal" and "most conservative" create caricatures with little, if any, useful meaning. Casting political battles as "fights to the finish" ensures that they will be. When citizens collaborate in solving problems such as public school reform, almost all evidence of a cultural split disappears and, along with it, much of our frustrating partisan process. Engaging citizens both inside and outside the government in what might be called "transpartisan integration" injects life into otherwise deadening politics.

Transpartisan Integration: Engaging Left and Right

In our view, Americans already seek political integration. They look for a unifying voice. They desire a way of seeing politics that nudges their inner dialogue toward society-enhancing engagement if not resolution. Here are some observations and suggestions on how people might pursue this integration. We hope these examples and this entire essay will provoke a public discourse on transpartisan politics.

Expand the Analyses

The starting place for a discourse on transpartisan politics, in our view, is to discard the current conservative/liberal spectrum. Sometimes people who rely on this spectrum treat order as conservative and freedom as liberal. We cannot make progress until we adopt a language that reveals huge differences within the left and within the right, not conceals them. This requires expanding and refining the terms "conservative" and "liberal" to a four-part freedom/order, left/right matrix. With such a matrix, political news stories, commentary, and even legislative initiatives might make more sense than the incessantly combative, narrow, partisan approach to political activities that is currently in vogue. The matrix creates a useful way to think about transpartisan politics by differentiating positions within the left and within the right that are, in fact, very different.

Transforming Taxes: A Transpartisan Discussion

Some ideas get lost because they do not fit the continuum: they are too big; they have too little partisan backing; they lack funding and connected advocates. Edgar L. Feige, emeritus professor of economics at the University of Wisconsin, Madison, proposes that all federal and state, personal and corporate income, sales and excise taxes, capital gains, import and export duties, and gift and estate taxes be replaced with a 0.06 percent transaction fee, or tax, on banking transactions, settled through the electronic technology of the banking/payments system.

On paper, this system, called the Automated Payment Transaction (APT)[1] tax, creates more government income than all the federal and state taxes currently collected. In addition "taxpayers would not," writes Chuck Martin of the *Wisconsin State Journal*, "have to spend what is now estimated to be $70 billion to $134 billion on preparing taxes. The government wouldn't lose the estimated $200 billion a year... it fails to collect because people cheat or make mistakes on tax returns" and would save the estimated $600 billion a year it takes to comply with and run our current tax system.[2]

Daniel Akst, writing in the *The New York Times*, calls the APT "a sort of tax-system E-Z Pass... enabling you to whiz through the [tax-paying] booths without an accountant in the back seat. ...

Mirror, mirror on the wall," he writes, "what's the fairest plan of all? My vote goes to the Automated Payment Transaction tax."[3]

The financial transaction tax offers a way of thinking about financing government that gives all Americans a chance to pay a very small sum to create more than enough money to run the federal and state governments. Furthermore, it offers a way for transpartisan politics to address large issues in new ways. We neither urge nor oppose adopting the APT. We do urge, however, broadening the political context to include space for serious consideration of this idea and others like it. Currently APT lacks enough advantage to any partisan political interest to receive serious consideration by the current political system.

Transpartisans who focus attention on ideas of this caliber serve the political system by opening the political arena to broader citizen action.

Expanding the Business/Commerce Context

Dee Hock, inventor of the Visa card, arguably America's most successful business, sets out a virtual owner's manual for transpartisan organizations in his Chaordics Movement.[4] The name *chaordic* integrates freedom and order. Hock designed Chaordics to apply the Visa principles — which have a transpartisan core — to all other arenas of American and global life.

FastCompany.com reporter, M. Mitchell Waldrop, writes: "The new [Visa] organization was indeed different — a nonstock, for-profit membership corporation with ownership in the form of nontransferable rights of participation. Hock designed the organization according to his philosophy: highly decentralized and highly collaborative. Authority, initiative, decision-making, wealth — everything possible is pushed out to the periphery of the organization, to the members. This design resulted from the need to reconcile a fundamental tension. On the one hand, the member financial institutions are fierce competitors: They — not Visa — issue the cards, which means they are constantly going after each other's customers. On the other hand, the members also have to cooperate with each other: For the system to work, participating merchants must be able to take any Visa card issued by any bank, anywhere.

"That means that the banks abide by certain standards on issues such as card layout. Even more important, they participate in a common clearinghouse operation, the system that reconciles all the accounts and makes sure merchants get paid for each purchase, the transactions are cleared between banks, and customers get billed."[5]

Dee Hock's integration of chaos and order creates a model for transpartisans to use in thinking about how to cooperate to preserve the strength of competition.

Synergizing Religion

The Abraham's Path initiative brings together Jews, Christians, and Muslims, using cultural tourism. More than half the world's population trace their history or faith back to Abraham, considered the father of monotheism — the common origin of Jewish, Christian, and Muslim religions.[6] The initiative began by organizing walking trips on the trail that tracks the life of Abraham, spiritual father of the three and a half billion members of the three monotheistic faiths. The trail covers 1,200 kilometers — from the Turkish city of Sanliurfa, apparent site of Abraham's birth — to the nearby ruins of Harran, where it is said Abraham heard God's call to go forth — to Abraham's tomb in the city of Hebron/Al-Khalil, just south of Jerusalem.

Now Abraham's Paths include local initiatives around the world. On April 2, 2006, three-hundred people from varying faiths participated in a nearly four-mile walk — starting at Cincinnati, Ohio's, New Thought Unity Church, then moving to a Jewish center, and ending at the Islamic Association of Cincinnati. Organizers of these events guide participants from churches to mosques to synagogues, sharing religious services and festivals, as well as holding educational events on religious co-existence.[7] Abraham's Path creates a sense of spiritual and religious integration that contributes another reference point to the transpartisan imperative.

This initiative illustrates the difference between coming up with a truce between conflicting religious beliefs and actually recognizing the deeply shared origins of the strongest commonly held beliefs. The recognition of common origins is a fundamental aspect of a transpartisan politics.

Fortunately, America's constitutional institutions create a "common origin" — a context for synergizing values, integrating cooperation and competition, designing a sound way to pay for public obligations, and recognizing the multifaceted ways in which liberals and conservatives can come together to search for freedom and order.

Empowering the American Transpartisan Imperative

Regardless of who takes the presidential oath of office, a huge transpartisan opportunity exists in America, in spite of partisan powers eager to continue to dominate national, state, and local politics.

Health care is an inefficient system with an enormous cost; we will need a great deal more than "universal insurance" to bring the needs of most people into congruence. Energy dependence will continue to distort policy in ways dangerous to the country. Education will still be plagued by dead schools and mechanical programs, no matter who wins our elections.

These realities create real opportunities for the 130 million Americans not aligned with, or wishing to transcend, both the Democratic and Republican partisans. Because public office holders are identified as either Republican or Democrat — groups that represent only thirty percent of the American populace — these partisans will need constant input from the large constituency that is unaffiliated with them or their parties. If there is another Gang of Fourteen organized to promote responsibility on the rules of the Senate, they should have constituents in their states who support them in that task.[8] If there is a Congressional retreat designed to return and retain civility in the House of Representatives, people from Congressional districts should support the initiative. As each public policy matter takes form in the legislative, regulatory, and judicial process, organized transpartisan constituents will have at their disposal all the mechanisms — government and non-government, public and private, individual and collective — built into the American constitutional process.

We suggest that a transpartisan politics "meet-up" be set up at http://www.meetup.com/ in each state house of representatives' legislative districts. These groups could communicate with each other through use of committees of correspondence to coordinate local, regional, state, and national political efforts. There could be more than one such group in each district. We recommend that these groups not endorse candidates. Let endorsements go to the partisans. Let the transpartisans seek out individuals from every political persuasion who want to talk with others of different persuasions. The objective is to build up interpersonal relationships focusing on public policy matters from throughout the political matrix. The two remaining presidential campaigns give a hint of the possibilities. The Obama campaign is linked to sixteen social networks into all of which it inserts its campaign message. Similarly, McCain is linked to more than fifty blogs organized by political orientation. These are powerful tools available to transpartisans as well as partisans.

As these groups begin to develop their relationships, they will build the kind of lobbying that has so helped special interests amass legislative power over the past several decades. The groups can pick issues and search for experts throughout the transpartisan political network. As the groups gain strength, they can begin to relate to and coordinate with their elected officials on the various matters that concern them. They can raise the funds for these activities on the Internet and in the other ways that politicians are noted for.

Reintegrating the transpartisan community into the political policy process is doable without the need either to embrace or forego participation in the political parties. Strong partisans can strengthen the transpartisan process they join. To facilitate this reintegration, groups are establishing transpartisan policy "salons" in Washington, DC, and other cities. They are creating a transpartisan book club, including publishing policy and process books on specific topics, and they are creating an active presence on the Internet.

The real change that everyone clamors for is actually happening.

CHAPTER ELEVEN

AN AWAKENED AMERICA

We believe that the partisan political debate, focused on our political capitals, mainstream media, and campaigns for public office, is profoundly out of touch with the character of our people. Evidence is all around us of voters profoundly alienated from the current political system:

> More Americans register to vote as independents or third-party voters than register for either "major" political party;
>
> More eligible voters fail to register than register as either Democratic or Republican; and
>
> In a poll by the Luntz Maslansky Group, eighty-one percent of the electorate stated they would consider voting for a third-party candidate.

These numbers represent a constituency of more than 130 million Americans — more than voted for president in 2004. Although such alienation raises serious concerns about our democratic future, it also offers real opportunity for change and progress.

People leave the partisan process out of disdain, disgust, and disinterest. They see the system as unresponsive, and un-representative of their interests. This is not a problem of candidates and constituents; it is a problem rooted in the structure of our political discourse.

The Changing Role of Leadership: Repairing the Structure of Partisan Politics

Our current politics is focused entirely on counting votes, money, and opinions. A sign in Albert Einstein's office cautioned about this obsession with numbers: "Not everything that can be counted counts, and not everything that counts can be counted." While mechanical systems are useful for many purposes, they are dead, and we think the main reason voters are turned off by our politics is that it is dead, too. Politics today is about people fighting with one another, people fearing each other, and people demonizing each other. It is a world that lacks the engagement or connection of organic or living systems.

Transpartisan politics seeks to broaden political discourse by importing the essential elements of living systems into politics — real engagement by political leaders with each other and real engagement, connection, and participation by citizens empowered to play active roles in public life. All of this will increase attention to the organic, living side of public and political life.

We have described two specific tools for doing this: 1) we urge expanding the two-part left/right spectrum for debate to a more robust four-part left/right-freedom/order matrix; and 2) beyond reformatting the debate, real operational progress depends upon creating institutions and leadership that reinvigorate the role of citizens in public spaces.

These two approaches will create an opportunity to recruit and engage large numbers of people currently opting out of the political system to join in the social work of the community. This will increase the numbers of participants in every phase of community activity, including voting.

To begin, we must build on what already exists — what has been shown to survive and triumph against unfriendly forces.

Recall Rick Roney's experiment on penal reform, promoting local ownership of the issue in Santa Barbara and ultimately gaining support from Sacramento. Recall the school reform strategy that Jim Dierke put in place at the Visitacion Valley Middle School in San Francisco.

Notice the role reversal of Al Gore and Ralph Nader. Political insider Gore rose to within 600 votes of winning the presidency, while Nader built a powerful citizen activist career. Then Nader ran for president, helping defeat Gore. It was like Michael Jordan playing baseball: a world-class player in the wrong game. Now citizen Gore has a Nobel Peace Prize, an Oscar, and more influence on environmental issues than he ever had as a public officeholder. Nader languishes, enmeshed in dead politics.

It is natural that citizens propel government in new directions. Governments designed to maintain order tend to *reflect* social and cultural innovation, rather than create and lead it. Citizens must be the source of that innovation. They must assign government's tasks: collecting garbage, plowing roads, ensuring enough safe food, shelter, and clothing, maintaining security, and securing individual rights.

Citizen movements drive change (*e.g.*, women's suffrage). Effective governments find ways to promote innovations produced by citizen initiatives and then incorporate them into public policy. Partisan governments fail at this. For government to manage change, we need a more collaborative model of leadership.

While citizen action is essential to move local, national, and global agendas forward, transpartisan leaders can play an important role in expanding programs — like Rick Roney's and Jim Dierke's — and encouraging development of other innovations. Political players like California Governor Arnold Schwarzenegger and New York City Mayor Michael Bloomberg should provide leadership in this new direction.

In announcing his decision not to run for president in 2008, Mayor Bloomberg wrote:

> The changes needed in this country are straight forward enough, but there are always partisan reasons to take an easy way out. There are always special interests that will fight against any challenge to the status quo. And there are always those who will worry more about their next election than the health of our country.
>
> These forces that prevent meaningful progress are powerful, and they exist in both parties. I believe that the candidate who recognizes that 'the party is over' and begins enlisting all of us to clean up the mess will be the winner this November, and will lead our country to a great and boundless future.'

We believe that whoever wins our national elections, an engaged transpartisan constituency is essential to the success of the American experiment and nation.

A transpartisan politics would generate many stories of cooperation, and we believe the media would report them. This would be especially true if media savvy political leaders themselves personally visited projects highlighting transpartisan collaboration (such as Rick Roney's penal reform project in Santa Barbara). The avalanche of press coverage generated by John McCain's April 2008 tour reaching out to African-Americans, displaced factory workers, and people living in poverty — voters not usually associated with the Republican Party — gives a sense of both the hunger of the American people for a different approach to campaigning and to governing. In campaigning, leaders can excite people by reaching out to a more diverse constituency. McCain went to Alabama's "Black Belt," then on to the struggling steel town of Youngstown, Ohio, the Appalachian region of Kentucky, and New Orleans, still recovering from 2005's Hurricane Katrina.

The theater of personal engagement can also be used to powerful effect in governing and leading, especially in highlighting innovative citizen initiatives in areas of social need. As an example, think of the effect if California Governor Arnold Schwarzenegger spent part of his time visiting successful, innovative public schools, learning how successful school communities work. He could do it in schools. He could visit the Santa Barbara penal reform project. He could visit businesses where people of different races and classes are working together, collaborating, and helping make the businesses succeed.

Besides visiting these community locations, he could also spend part of his time visiting state bureaucratic agencies and showcasing examples of how state workers and bureaucrats are working to empower citizens to help solve their own problems. Some people may be skeptical that he could find such positive examples of bureaucratic action. But if he embraced this new model, he could actively encourage government officials to play a new role, and he could reward them for doing so.

Such an approach would require great imagination. To succeed, it would require careful preparation, especially in promoting initiatives that appeared inside the government agencies so they could own them. The important point is that the theater of personal engagement would attract excited citizen participation and swarming media attention. Encouraged by wide media coverage, political leaders could perform an incredible service in educating the public about what is possible.

Only organic approaches that engage people will generate workable solutions to persistent problems. People in all regions of the world are assuming increasingly conscious roles in community life. They are redefining themselves and repositioning themselves to become effectively involved citizens – citizen actors who integrate with collaborative leaders and animate transpartisan politics.

Failure to grasp this engaged, organic context renders meaningless all calculations and numbers by pollsters, politicians, and the media. Understanding this new and evolving context, however, gives the numbers powerful meaning.

The Paradox of Political Change

A paradoxical logic underlying large policy changes provides an important motivator for a transpartisan politics. When Nixon, the quintessential anticommunist, went to China, that event became the archetypal example of this paradoxical logic.

The logic is pretty simple. In most policy debates, one party proposes reform and the other party opposes it. Examples are everywhere. Republicans want to reform Social Security; Democrats oppose reform. Democrats want to cut defense spending; Republicans oppose cuts.

The temptation to ignore paradoxical logic can be very strong when one political party controls both the executive and legislative branches of a government. They have the power, so they push their own solution and crush their "enemy." But paradoxical logic is most obvious on issues that are very large and controversial – issues that one party cannot carry out on its own. When change does happen, it is because the opposing party embraces, if not initiates, the change and unites the political culture behind it.

The logic becomes obvious in reviewing the history of major policy changes. Remember what President Kennedy and the Democrats did in 1962, when they actually cut taxes on the rich to stimulate the economy and to reduce incentives for people to hide their incomes.

When Jimmy Carter was president, he had to work with a Congress controlled in both houses by his own party. Because of uncontrolled spending, the economy careened out of control to the point where he had to run for re-election in 1980 with inflation above ten percent and interest rates at twenty percent. Concern among his advisors about runaway spending was so great that his legal advisor, Lloyd Cutler, proposed publicly that we move constitutionally to a parliamentary system to help control spending.

As governor of California (for eight years) and as president (for eight years), Reagan faced legislatures controlled by the Democrats. He achieved some extraordinary legislative accomplishments in both periods, always reaching across the aisle and negotiating solutions with bipartisan leadership and bipartisan credit. In Sacramento, he and Bob Moretti, the Democratic speaker of the State Assembly, appeared in public to announce their landmark welfare reform legislation and also their reform of the state's medical care system. These were Governor Reagan's greatest legislative achievements. In Washington, Reagan worked with Tip O'Neill, Speaker of the House, and also with Congressman Rostenkowski, chairman of the House Ways and Means Committee (with the latter especially on reducing the highest personal income tax rates from seventy to fifty percent — a reform first proposed by the Democrats in 1981).

Reagan had been a liberal Democrat until 1960, helping to found the liberal Americans for Democratic Action, had campaigned for Hubert Humphrey for public office, and had a similar transpartisan impact in international affairs. When protesters wanted to freeze nuclear weapons, Reagan countered with reducing the number of such weapons.

Max Kampelman, who identifies himself as a longtime liberal Democrat in the Hubert Humphrey tradition, was arms negotiator for both Presidents Carter and Reagan. He found Reagan to be quite open on arms control, as the following story shows: At one meeting with the president, his advisors all cautioned against a proposal Kampelman advanced on arms control. He reports that Reagan, "sensing disappointment I did not feel, spoke up.

'Don't pay any attention to these fellows, Max,' he said. 'Not a single one of them was ever a Democrat!'"

Both Ronald Reagan and Bill Clinton were fortunate to serve as president while working with a Congress controlled by the other party. For six of his eight years as president, Bill Clinton was fortunate to face a Republican Congress, with which he accomplished his most important legislative achievements. During this period, Congress passed his landmark welfare reform, spending was controlled, and the economy boomed. While working with a Republican Congress, Clinton was able to pursue a "Third Way" philosophy that sought to adapt progressive values to the challenges of the information age. The Third Way, as practiced by Bill Clinton and Tony Blair, was a step beyond bipartisan but still not yet transpartisan.

Political leaders ignore the paradoxical logic of policy reform at their peril. If they do not control both houses of the legislature, they must work cooperatively with the other party. Many conservatives and Republicans are convinced today that the Democrats have moved far to the left and now oppose positions they always supported in the past, such as free trade. We believe, however, that current statements by Democrats may be a poor indicator of what they would do in office.

We think that liberals and Democrats are so angry at Bush, who they believe has moved so far to the right, that opposition to him and his policies has become a metaphor for their rage. If so, their current voting record and statements may be a poor indicator of what they would do if they were in office, especially if conditions forced them to cooperate with Republicans.

Nixon going to China is the archetypal example, but there are many examples of paradoxical logic, such as military base closings, welfare reform, the enactment of Social Security, and most major New Deal reforms. Paradoxical logic also applies in other countries:

- Gorbachev, a Communist, bringing down Communism in the USSR
- De Klerk, an old supporter of apartheid ending that practice in South Africa
- Teng Hsiao-Ping, a Communist, introducing major elements of capitalism into China

It is difficult to think of a single, major reform being enacted without the support of, and even leadership from, the "opposition."

It is important to note again here why this paradoxical logic is part of the transpartisan rather than bipartisan vision. Bipartisan is about mechanical compromises. Transpartisan is about empowerment: of people as citizens, of political parties and ideological groups, and even of countries.

The seemingly paradoxical logic of reform suggests important things about which strategies will work in addressing really difficult issues, such as health insurance, Medicare, Social Security, education, energy, and defense spending.

Again, major reforms tend to happen when the opponent of a reform embraces the reform, unites the country, and implements the reform. Opponents of particular policy reforms tend to control how much of what they oppose gets on the public agenda.

Active Citizenship: Organizing Transpartisan Political Campaigns

At the present time, citizens' roles in most public life are limited to participating in elections — working in campaigns, raising money, registering voters, and voting. One might say this is like a series of sprints, except that the election season is now approaching a full-time job, and citizens are now running marathons.

We think voters are alienated because they haven't been seriously involved. The system lets them select the leaders and relegates them, as Robert Hawkins puts it, to the role of consumers: consuming services provided by the government. They want more than this passive role. They want an active role in designing, and also in implementing, policies in a variety of areas. A transpartisan politics would give them that role.

Imagine a world in which citizens initiated innovative programs in education, penal reform, community development, even reforms affecting other countries through foreign policy initiatives. Imagine playing a role in both designing and implementing these projects.

Like Rick Roney's penal reform program in Santa Barbara, some of the initiatives would provide tangible benefits to local communities; others would not.

These activities would create new connections and new ideas for projects. Roney's penal reform project, for example, led naturally to a general prison reform initiative that combined the conservatives' desire to build new prisons with the liberals' focus on rehabilitation.

These independent initiatives would create an independent base for change, which could both help elected officials pass key legislation and press them to act more strongly when tempted to compromise too easily. Such initiatives would also reserve an important role for citizens in implementation.

Imagine political campaigns that relied on volunteers to organize themselves, take their own initiative, and find strength in connecting with each other. Imagine campaigns ensuring that every critical precinct gets walked, and every key household gets called – campaigns that stayed focused on "the message" by encouraging volunteers to talk about their reasons for participating. This is the way Paul Loeb describes the Barak Obama presidential primary campaign of 2008.

Writing in *The New York Times* on March 5, 2008, the day of the key Texas and Ohio presidential primaries, conservative columnist David Brooks identified a speech given by Obama on

November 10, 2007, as the pivotal moment of the 2008 presidential primaries. First, Brooks contrasted the Hillary Clinton and Obama approaches. Clinton had "used 'fight' or 'fought' fifteen times in one passage of the speech," Brooks reported.

"Instead of waging a partisan campaign as Clinton had just done," Brooks wrote, "Obama vowed to address not just Democrats, but Republicans and independents who've lost trust in their government but want to believe again. 'The same old Washington textbook campaigns just won't do,'" he quoted Obama as saying.

Then he describes the historical moment. "[T]his is a country," he wrote, "in the midst of a crisis of authority, a country that has become disillusioned not only with one president, but with a whole system of politics. It's a country that has lost faith not only with one institution, but with the entire set of leadership institutions." The cultural context, in other words, allowed for a much broader critique, a much more audacious vocabulary than Clinton's, "and Barack Obama leapt right in," Brooks asserted, "setting the tone for the 2008 primaries and beyond."

In the same vein, notice the difference between what the country expected from the primaries on January 1, 2008, and what actually happened. Four candidates, two from each party — three senators and one former governor — remained technically viable in the race for president until March. All four candidates found themselves in positions strikingly different from what observers expected.

All four either embraced or reacted to, in one degree or another, what Brooks describes as "Obama's theory of social change...This theory," Brooks says, "turns business-as-usual, top-down management on its head...Obama, in the climactic passage of his speech," Brooks writes, "described how change bubbles from the bottom-up: 'And because that somebody stood up, a few more stood up. And then a few thousand stood up. And then a few million stood up. And standing up, with courage and clear purpose, they somehow managed to change the world!'"

Now relate what happened in the 2008 primaries to a plan to actualize the transpartisan imperative. The plan might include creating a transpartisan club in each political jurisdiction. People in state legislatures, city councils, or county government districts could meet regularly. Republicans, Democrats, third-party members, independents, and unregistered residents who want to participate would meet to take positions, plan actions, and support transpartisan initiatives from other such clubs around the country.

There are several possibilities how such clubs might develop. They might form around associations that are already widely organized, such as civic groups, business organizations, or labor and church groups. We believe some people in organized politics, who are now active partisans, may wish to enjoy the benefits of running as transpartisans, and when they do, they too will work actively to organize clubs supporting them.

These clubs follow the tradition of the eighteenth-century Committees of Correspondence, which laid the theoretical and organizational groundwork for the American Revolution. They share characteristics with the Metaphysical Club in the late nineteenth-century in Cambridge, Massachusetts, which developed important proposals for educational, legal, and electoral reforms.[2] They look like the thousands of post-World War II citizens groups that formed the backbone of the civil rights, consumer, environmental, women's and other citizen movements that have helped shape policy on a variety of important issues.

In taking avowedly transpartisan positions, these institutions would be different from issue-oriented citizen advocacy groups. For one thing, they would not endorse candidates. Because they developed their proposals in transpartisan collaboration, they would avoid the demonization and blame that infects so many political advocacy groups. Most importantly, they would organize the constituencies that would implement transpartisan initiatives and/or demand a more collaborative style of politics from candidates and office-holders.

During the 1990s, an initiative to promote a transpartisan politics revealed both the opportunities and the great difficulties associated with inside institutions addicted to partisanship and conflict. The initiative was organized and led by facilitator and organizer Mark Gerzon, and it led to two highly successful, bipartisan Congressional retreats. But while the participants were greatly energized by the transpartisan comity the retreats promoted, the Congressional leadership of both parties blocked additional retreats involving their members. The initiative continued with participation of Congressional staff, but lacking participation of the members, the retreats ended soon after they began.

A similar kind of effort surfaced briefly in 2005 and 2006, when the "Gang-of-Fourteen" U.S. Senators — seven Democratic and seven Republican — organized to block partisan filibusters on judicial nominees. Constituencies of transpartisan clubs in the home districts of members of Congress could exert pressure to continue such activities, reconstitute the retreats, and initiate other, similar events. In today's information world, organizing and funding a national net-work of transpartisan clubs seems entirely doable. Meet-ups and other social networking Internet sites offer the tools to create such groups. "Real groups make a real difference" is the slogan of MeetUps, the premier Internet networking site, which held 74,000 meetings in March of 2008. *Time Magazine* called it "a convenient, non-threatening way to connect to other people who share similar interests and live nearby." *The Toronto Sun* says: "[I]t's important to stay true to your passions or interests, whatever they may be... An opportunity to reconnect with yourself and others in a stress-free environment. It's as simple as that." These are the principles of transpartisan engagement.

The last two presidential campaigns demonstrated the power of political organizations to raise funds using the Internet. Candidates in the 2008 primaries are constantly breaking monthly fund raising records, creating the most costly and the most broadly financed presidential campaigns in history. Candidates for other offices are finding the Internet an effective fund raising tool, as well. It can also become an essential tool for transpartisan clubs.

What's needed are places where citizens can act in more public, political, less-partisan ways than is possible in a typical social club. Individuals in transpartisan clubs need not abandon their partisan allegiances. Indeed, the transpartisan clubs would work most effectively when some members also remain members of partisan organizations. Actions across partisan lines will give voice to the newly-engaged citizen activist.

The world's citizens feel the frustration of being ignored by their political representatives but now have the technology to communicate directly with anyone, everywhere, at any time. By connecting the "humanness" in all of us, transpartisan impulses will begin to shake, then topple, the archaic partisan biases that stand in the way of solving our greatest problems and, as a result, will seek to powerfully align the healthy self-interests of us all.

Conclusion
Leadership for a New Politics

With 130 million potential voters currently opting out of partisan politics and increasing numbers leaving the major parties and becoming independents, our political system is in crisis. We have argued that people are unhappy with politics because it's all about power. They are also unhappy because the current system disempowers them and leaves them no room, as citizens, to play meaningful roles in solving major public issues.

Americans are seeking ways of pursuing a politics broader and more vibrant than the current system. We present this "manifesto" for a transpartisan politics to reinvigorate citizenship and reduce conflict.

Our argument moves through three principal stages:

- Expanding the current left-right political spectrum into a left-right/freedom-order matrix, highlighting the creative tension between freedom and order within both the left and right;

- Creating a new conceptual framework for integrating freedom and order – an organic framework drawing on the essence of both conservative and liberal political traditions that is broader and less static than the terms of the current debate permit; and finally,

- Promoting a new, empowered form of citizenship that uses civic engagement and human relationships to provide leadership to strengthen institutions and solve problems that now seem beyond solution.

Our first stage reconstructs the current left-right political spectrum into "freedom" and "order" components on both "left" and "right." This point follows the argument made by A. Lawrence Chickering in his 1993 book, *Beyond Left and Right*, that hiding the conflicts between freedom and order on both the left and right reduces the terms "conservative" and "liberal" to incoherence. The political debate is much better described by four positions rather than two: a freedom and an order position for both left and right. This model untangles the contradictions and provides a much better guide for understanding political arguments and predicting political positions.

The important point is that there are enormous unresolved conflicts within the left and within the right. These conflicts are an effort to reconcile and integrate the two great values of all modern societies: freedom and order.*

Some people prefer the more common words "rights" and "responsibilities" to the words "freedom" and "order." However, using "rights and responsibilities" misses an essential point in the argument. The modern mechanistic emphasis on rights has all but extinguished the moral authority of traditional responsibilities. Rights and responsibilities are interdependent because rights depend on corresponding responsibilities. Nonetheless, in the current political debate people commonly say, imprecisely we believe, that we must "balance" rights and responsibilities.

We believe that "rights" and "responsibilities" remain extremely important in legal and moral systems. However, the freedom/order framework we advocate creates broader understanding of new possibilities for responsibility. The framework we urge has been shown, in all regions of the world, greatly to increase the responsibility people feel for each other. Our proposal is to create spaces that encourage people voluntarily to reach out to each other in common purpose. This will happen especially in self-governing institutions, in which people will freely choose to be obligated. The more of these spaces we create, the more "moral behavior" and what in more traditional times was called "character" will be revealed voluntarily, and the less we will have to depend on mechanistic appeals to responsibilities, either legal or moral. The spirit of our ambition to create these new spaces requires words that are completely neutral and broadly embraced—hence "freedom" and "order".

The integration puzzle has not been solved. Until it is, the dialectical tension between freedom and order will persist, and incoherence will continue to dominate our political debate. The narrow and brittle left-right continuum currently in use describes only the mechanistic political world that is generating so much unhappiness. We propose the four-part, left/right-freedom/order matrix to lay the groundwork for solving the integration puzzle. Unless we first highlight the problem, we conceal the limitations in the current spectrum and we obstruct creation of a connected, organic vision that would really humanize politics and bring the people actively into political life.

The second theme in our transpartisan vision is to critique the mechanistic habits of thinking that have dominated Western thought for at least three centuries. Our purpose is not to reject philosophical mechanism; we affirm the importance of mechanistic forms of thinking, which have been essential to many fields, especially science and medicine. We believe, however, that the attempt to use mechanistic thinking as the dominant, if not exclusive, element in studying human relationships and societies has had extremely negative consequences. It has brutalized public institutions, often immobilizing people whose path to change is through hope in the future rather than looking back at the "causes" of dysfunction. The relentless use of mechanistic tools in management of public schools, for example, has caused many of them to be frozen and desiccated by bureaucratic rules and mechanistic cultures.

Neither the left nor the right has understood the full dimensions of this tragedy, because both sides have been influenced and even dominated by mechanistic thinking. (The debate between state and market is at a dead end because positions of both "left" and "right" are almost entirely mechanistic.) Organic ways of seeing the world have advanced furthest in the debate on the environment and on the "green" imperative. It is much easier to argue for organic modes of thought today than it would have been, say, fifty years ago. However, it is important, again, to be clear that we are not arguing for organic rather than mechanistic; we are arguing for an appreciation of both, in their distinct spheres of value.

The heart of the issue of organic versus mechanical is best expressed in the question of whether we believe in a connected world, or not. Mechanistic systems are unconnected and dead. Organic systems are connected and alive. Trying to understand human beings and their relationships exclusively in mechanistic terms reduces us all to robots. Raising the dead by breathing life into institutions that have gone dead happens wherever institutions are organized and run with a deep commitment to the importance of creating connected, organic cultures within them.

Belief in a connected world is the central imperative that underlies our struggles to reform public schools, to solve the continuing tragedy of race, and even to address, in a serious way, the problem of deteriorating health and persistent poverty. It is central to finding solutions to the new challenges of national security after 9/11. None of these problems can be solved without understanding the need for powerful, connected civic engagement: bringing people together in a way that they simply are not at the present time... not even close.

Everybody knows in private that this vision of redemption in engaged, connected life is true. Now we need to bring it into the public square. Its truth is obvious from examining the great majority of social experiments that are working in all regions of the world, with every race, religion, and class.

Integration of freedom and order is only possible in a connected world. It is only possible in a world that is alive. The current debate is consumed by mechanistic arguments about state versus market. A world without engagement and connection is a world that is lost. In many ways, that describes the state of public spaces in our world today. Again, the contrast to private life is striking and tragic.

The attraction of the "dark side" of faction and ego may be in our nature, but the antidote is also in our nature: the impulse to connect, cooperate, and engage. This antidote has, again, always been powerful in private life. The great need today is to make it also powerful in public life.

The commitment to organic (alive) in place of mechanical (dead) provides the philosophical key to integrating freedom and order, to bringing people back together politically, and to restoring coherence to our political debate. The final theme describes how this connected, engaged conceptual worldview looks in the real world: how it would inform a new, transpartisan politics.

This connected worldview appears in the world as a strong concept of citizenship. It replaces the weak concept, made weak by mechanistic institutions. It creates institutions that promote strong citizenship by empowering and engaging citizens to play significant roles in public spaces. It supports leaders who understand that an engaged, transpartisan politics is about "the People" (as explained in Lincoln's words about our Constitution: "of the people, by the people, for the people"), not about themselves. In this vision, the leader's challenge is to promote development of self-governing institutions that empower citizens and engage them in common purpose. Such institutions will promote the engaged citizenship that will allow every citizen to realize the full potential of their contribution to their country, their community, their family, and themselves. These institutions will provide to every leader essential resources for solving seemingly intractable problems.

Starting a Conversation

We have written this essay to start a conversation. We do not claim to have all the answers. We do believe we are raising significant questions. We hope others will join us and help us fill in the blanks. In the past, *Great Leaders* told us, with great confidence, what was *True*. We think much of what is true going forward will be about how people engage each other and rediscover spirit in a largely mechanistic public world.

We think the conflict in our political life has become brutal and counterproductive. We think this conflict is provoked by the brittle political structure that surrounds us and is more between political insiders and people demanding to be engaged rather than among groups of "the people" (*e.g.*, red and blue) themselves. We think this struggle has happened in part because many of our institutions, especially our public institutions, have failed to bring people together and connect them and are, instead, disempowering and separating them, individually and collectively.

We have lost the meaning of "public." "Public" should refer to civic space in which citizens, in government and the private sector, come together and engage each other to work on the major issues we face: health, education, security, and so on. Instead, "public" has come to mean "government," and "government" has come to describe an institution of rights and rules that mechanically mediates material relations among people while marginalizing the essentials of personal relationships. In this mechanical world, the rights and rules are sovereign, faint echoes of the role played by religious dogma in earlier times, and when this happens, freedom, trust, and spirit weaken and often disappear.

The American founders worried about faction, which they believed is in our nature. The impulses to cooperation and connection are also, however, in our nature and in our founding institutions. A central challenge for leadership is to encourage these non-factious impulses by revitalizing institutions that empower and engage people.

Politics in the democratic tradition is meant to help reduce, not exploit, conflicts. It should promote a strong concept of citizenship, not the weak concept we have today. While many people blame teachers' unions and public employee unions for the decline of public spirit in public institutions, we believe these unions have become strong and combative in recent decades because bureaucratic public institutions have disempowered and brutalized their members (public school teachers and public employees), all but destroying the prestige they enjoyed in earlier times when they had real authority, real respect from citizens, and real connections with them.[1]

American politics today has turned the traditional purpose of politics, building society by encouraging strong citizenship, on its head, and has replaced it with a society-deadening exploitation of conflict, often tangential conflict at that, by grabbing political power for power's sake.

The key to public spirit cannot be found in disconnected abstract appeals to large visions. It appears and grows most powerfully in private engagement, especially in engagements across the lines of class, race, gender, nationality, and politics — especially partisan politics — across all of the differences that are now the subject of such concern. Private engagement is even more powerful when it takes place in the context of large connected visions.

It is time that people of all political types start reaching out to one another using our shared humanity to weave a social tapestry that includes our differences to engage each other in common purpose.

There is enormous work to be done, not only in our country, but throughout the world. Our best hope for beginning to do what needs doing demands that we come together now, joining our best efforts to form the relationships that give meaning to life and life to our society.

It is time to begin. Tomorrow comes.

Postscript

DO YOU HEAR THE PEOPLE SING?

One of the greatest novels ever written, made into one of the most popular musicals ever sung, Victor Hugo's 1862 novel *Les Misérables*, which chronicles the effort to bring "the people" into French politics in the early 1800s, features the anthem "Do You Hear the People Sing." This song captures one form of the Voice of the People. While set in France with violence as its motif, it captures the essence of the people of America, even though we Americans replace violence with voting as our measure of domestic political victory. Here are the key lyrics in print and four Internet locations where you can hear and see the song sung in different settings, followed by the last sung words of three of the main characters:

ENJOLRAS

Do you hear the people sing?
Singing a song of angry men?
It is the music of a people
Who will not be slaves again!
When the beating of your heart
Echoes the beating of the drums
There is a life about to start
When tomorrow comes!

COMBEFERRE
Will you join in our crusade?
Who will be strong and stand with me?
Beyond the barricade
Is there a world you long to see?-
Courfeyrac
Then join in the fight
That will give you the right to be free!

*   *   *

CAST

http://uk.youtube.com/watch?
v=x6-5g78Nr6Q&feature=related

10 ANNIVERSARY ENSEMBLE

http://uk.youtube.com/watch?
v=VCYr8TWAGno&feature=related

TENORS FROM 17 DIFFERENT COUNTRIES

http://uk.youtube.com/watch?
v=KPpkTgMbhRU

RON PAUL

http://uk.youtube.com/watch?
v=Y6pAcBXt2j8

VALJEAN, FANTINE, EPONINE

Remember
The truth that once was spoken
To love another person
Is to see the face of God.

*   *   *

Appendix

I

Individuals who attended Reuniting America meetings over the past four years held key positions in groups representing more than 30 million Americans. People who served on the steering committee of Reuniting American held leadership positions in the following organizations:

American Association for
    Affirmative Action
American Conservative Union
Americans for Tax Reform
American Gas Association
American Legion
America Speaks
America Votes
BrainTrain
Center for a New
    American Dream
Christian Coalition
Club for Growth
Common Cause
Constitution Project
Conversation Café
Council for Excellence in
Government
Deep Dialogues for
    Deep Democracy
Democracy in America Project
Equal Rights Advocates
Fetzer Institute

Foundation for
    Conscious Evolution
Global Citizens Journey
Global Negotiation Project,
    Harvard Law School
League of Woman Voters
Lets Talk America
Liberty Coalition
Mediators Foundation
Meetup.com
Momsrising.org
Muslim Public Affairs Council
National Commons
National Council of Churches
    USA
Patrick Henry Center
Patriots to Restore
    Checks and Balances
Public Conversations Project
Search for Common Ground
    USA
Utne Institute
Utne Magazine

II

An important part of the conversation we are encouraging is to define what 'transpartisan' means. We know people will have different definitions and will also react differently to this list. We find it significant and interesting how many organizations were willing to identify *themselves* as transpartisan in response to a questionnaire that begins the process of creating an online directory of such groups on the Transpartisan Voice website:

1. MEDIATORS FOUNDATION

For the past twenty years Mediators Foundation has been an incubator for transpartisan initiatives in the United States and an advocate for such work around the world. Through its president Mark Gerzon, it served as co-designer and chief facilitator of the Bipartisan Congressional Retreats in 1997 and 1999. It provided early support to America Speaks, acted as the fiscal agent and nonprofit incubator for Reuniting America, and has underwritten numerous other transpartisan activities.

> Mark Gerzon, Mediators Foundation
> 525 Arapahoe Avenue, Suite E-4 #509
> Boulder, Colorado 80302
> TEL 303 444-1854

2. EAST WEST INSTITUTE

This foreign policy think tank, based in New York, Brussels and Moscow, has quietly played a transpartisan role for the past quarter century. With a board consisting of both Republicans and Democrats, as well as non-Americans of widely divergent political perspectives, it has worked closely with all administrations to develop a values-based, pragmatic, transpartisan perspective on the most challenging geopolitical issues. A key "Track II diplomacy" bridge between Moscow and Washington during the Cold War, it continues to play a similar behind-the-scenes role today among the major powers.

> Jean Dumont, East West Institute

700 Broadway, 2nd floor
New York, New York 10003
TEL 212 824-4100

3. AMERICASPEAKS

AmericaSpeaks is a nonprofit organization with the mission of providing citizens with a greater voice on the most important decisions that impact their lives. Over the past decade, AmericaSpeaks has convened more than 130,000 citizens in facilitated deliberations to identify collective priorities on issues like health care reform, regional economic development and disaster recovery after Hurricane Katrina and the attacks of September 11.

Carolyn Lukensmeyer, President and Founder
1050 17th Street, Ste. 350
Washington, DC 20036
TEL 202 775-3939

4. U.S. CONSENSUS COUNCIL/SEARCH FOR COMMON GROUND-USA

Under the auspices of Search for Common Ground-USA, the U.S. Consensus Council has organized several policy consensus-building projects on issues of national importance, including ones on health care coverage for the uninsured (HCCU) and on U.S.-Muslim Engagement (USME). The central approach has been to build agreements for action among people and organizations in leadership roles who have the knowledge, experience and influence to have an impact once an agreement is reached. The results have been broadly supportable recommendations and new coalitions for action that cut across normal partisan lines.

Robert Fersh (rfersh@sfcg.org) or
Susan Koscis (skoscis@sfcg.org)

Search for Common Ground
1601 Connecticut Avenue
NW, Washington, DC, 20009

202 265-4300 www.sfcg-usa.org
TEL 202 777-2229 | FAX 202 232-6718

5. ABRAHAM PATH INITIATIVE

The Abraham Path Initiative seeks to build mutual understanding and respect between the West and the global Muslim community by creating a permanent route of cultural tourism in the Middle East that retraces the footsteps of Abraham, the unifying figure of Judaism, Christianity, and Islam. The Abraham Path is a route of cultural tourism that retraces the journey made by Abraham (Ibrahim) through the heart of the Middle East some four thousand years ago. Three and a half billion people — over half the human family — trace their history or faith back to Abraham, considered the father of monotheism. The Abraham Path honors this shared cultural heritage by linking together into a single itinerary of outstanding interest and beauty the ancient sites associated with Abraham and his family.

> Abraham Path Initiative
> 1245 Pearl Street, Suite 208
> Boulder CO 80302
> TEL 303 447-8326
> www.abrahampath.org | info@abrahampath.org

6. E-PARLIAMENT

If we could spread good laws like these to more countries, we might get global warming under control. But how can it be done quickly enough? The e-Parliament links the world's democratic parliamentary representatives for the first time into a single forum, online and in person, to share ideas and implement policy on common issues such as reversing climate change and providing clean energy for all. The e-Parliament can play a similar role on other issues as well. Through this new global forum, legislators are working together to promote democracy and freedom of expression, and examining security issues brought about by the development of weapons in space. We welcome ideas on social policy and the economy. Whether you are a legislator, an organization or an individual citizen, you are welcome to participate. Together, we can make a difference.

> info@e-parl.net

7. THE MAINSTREAM MEDIA PROJECT and
A WORLD of POSSIBILITIES, INC.

Founded in 1995, the Mainstream Media Project (MMP) is a nonprofit public education and strategic communications organization that uses the mainstream broadcast media to raise public awareness about new approaches to longstanding societal problems. MMP pursues its public education mission through two complementary programs:

> 1. The Guests on Call program issues media alerts pegged to breaking news events to regional and national radio markets, booking radio interviews with experts, analysts, stakeholders and on-the-ground practitioners.

> 2. The award-winning, nationally and internationally syndicated radio program, "A World of Possibilities," features leading policy analysts and social innovators from around the world addressing key global issues.

A World of Possibilities, Inc., is a social innovation catalyst, a nonprofit organization that gathers and disseminates through a range of old and new media the most compelling stories of successful innovation for public benefit. It maintains a social innovation exchange that enables users to find other innovators working in the same fields, collaborate in designing solutions to shared challenges, and link up with potential investors to take their initiatives to scale. It takes a both/and approach to problems, assuming that none has the whole answer but many have parts to contribute.

> Mark Sommer, Executive Director
> 854 Ninth Street, Suite B
> Arcata, CA 95521
> TEL 707-826-9111, ext. 12 | CELL 707-498-6512
> www.aworldofpossibilities.com
> mark@mainstream-media.net

9. ELEANOR LeCAIN — author of *Breakthrough Solutions Which Can Improve Your Life and Change the World, with an Introduction by His Holiness the Dalai Lama,* and president of World Innovation Network — has the mission of working with individuals and groups to help build a new world by convening positive visions of what is possible in individual lives and society and providing strategies for strengthening the capacity of organizations and government agencies to design and implement plans of action for positive change.

http://www.worldinnovationnetwork.org/Crime.html

Here are two examples from her book:

A. DELANCEY STREET: Delancey Street is a highly successful rehabilitation center based in San Francisco, where, using a model of social entrepreneurship, education, rehabilitation and change that is exciting and full of hope, criminals and drug addicts can turn their lives around and become productive citizens at no cost to the taxpayer. It is the country's leading residential self-help organization for former substance abusers, ex-convicts, homeless and others, ranging from teenagers to senior citizens, including men and women and all races and ethnicities who have hit bottom. Started in 1971 with four people in a San Francisco apartment, Delancey Street has served many thousands of residents, in five locations throughout the United States.

http://www.delanceystreetfoundation.org
Delancey Street San Francisco
600 Embarcadero San Francisco, CA 94107
TEL 415-512-5104 | FAX 415-512-5141

B. CENTRAL PARK EAST: Deborah Meier founded a public high school in East Harlem called Central Park East where 90 percent of the students graduate and about 90 percent of the graduates go to college. Meier, a visionary teacher whose work has had a profound effect on education in New York City and the nation, founded Central Park East in 1974. Her belief that schools should be small, humane, democratic places where children learn how to learn and how to think for themselves helped spark a revival of progressive education in the city and the nation. It's hard to imagine how revolutionary Central Park East and its two sister schools, Central Park East II and River East, were when they first opened — and how much influence they've had on education in the past two decades.

http://www.insideschools.org/fs/school_profile.php?id=1166

Central Park East I
1573 Madison Avenue
New York, NY 10029
TEL (212) 860-5821 | FAX(212) 860-6017
Principal: Julie Zuckerman

C. ROCKY MOUNTAIN INSTITUTE: Amory Lovins is a leading world energy expert whose advice is sought by groups ranging from energy companies to the U.S. Department of Energy and Defense to 50 governments worldwide. He co-founded and leads the Rocky Mountain Institute in Colorado, an independent, market-oriented, nonprofit applied research center. His energy efficiency plan may carry more traction given that it was partially funded by the Pentagon. Lovins provides a roadmap to U.S. energy independence in his latest book, Wining the Oil Endgame: Innovation for Profits, Jobs, and Security. He shows how we can cut our dependence on oil by combining innovative technologies, new business models, and a fresh approach to public policies. His approach is market-oriented and does not require major national legislation.

http://www.rmi.org/sitepages/pid23.php

Rocky Mountain Institute	Rocky Mountain Institute
2317 Snowmass Creek Road	1820 Folsom Street
Snowmass, Colorado 81654	Boulder, Colorado 80302
TEL 970 927-3851	TEL 303 245-1003

III

Journalist Mark Satin, who has participated in and reported on beyond left and right initiatives for three decades, responded to the request for inclusion in the Transpartisan Voice web directory, saying:

RADICAL MIDDLE ONLINE NEWSLETTER

Radical Middle Online Newsletter, founded in 1999, publishes original, carefully researched articles on public policy issues. It is transpartisan because its articles typically merge good ideas from many political perspectives to come up with creative and integrative policy proposals − *e.g.*, universal preventive health care, income-based affirmative action, prudent globalization.

1. See the 25 "Red Hot Radical Middle Initiatives" on http://www.radicalmiddle.com

Ashoka

Breakthrough Institute

Center for Global Development

Centrist Coalition

Committee for a Responsible Federal Budget

Communitarian Network

Consensus Building Institute

Environmental Defense

Ethical Markets

Giraffe Heroes Project

Global Business Network

Information Technology & Innovation Foundation

Institute for Alternative Futures

National Coalition for Dialogue and Deliberation

NDN/New Politics Institute

New America Foundation

Progressive Policy Institute

Republican Main Street Partnership

RESULTS

Reuniting America
Search for Common Ground
Third Way
Unity08
Vasconcellos Project
World Future Society

2. See the more than 250 additional organizations listed under the categories World Order, Business and Economics, Energy and Environment, Health and Health Care, Education and Youth, Society and Futures, Politics and Process under the "Politics and Process" heading on:

http://www.radicalmiddle.com/organizations.htm

Radical Middle Online Newsletter
http://www.radicalmiddle.com
Contact Mark Satin (editor)
msatin@radicalmiddle.com or
P.O. Box 70188
Oakland, CA 94612

Endnotes

FOREWORD

1   The Transpartisan Center and Democracy in America work under the umbrella of *Reuniting America*, an unincorporated, open-source network of individuals, associations and organizations engaged in transpartisan dialogue. To learn more about Voice of the People and other Transpartisan initiatives go to Transpartisan Voice:

INTRODUCTION AND OVERVIEW

1   Don Edward Beck, PhD of the Center for Values & Culture, Denton, Texas, and author of *Spiral Dynamics: Mastering Values, Leadership and Change*, prepared a report titled "Centrism in a Transpartisan World, An Integral Strategy for President-Elect George W. Bush," addressing some of these issues in preparation for Bush inauguration day 2001.

PART I - THE CRISIS IN OUR POLITICS: PARTISAN FATIGUE

1   PollingReport.com CONGRESS — Job Rating in national polls
http://www.pollingreport.com/CongJob.htm

2   PollingReport.com PRESIDENT BUSH — Overall Job Rating in national polls http://www.pollingreport.com/BushJob.htm

3   Want to take back our country from partisan politics and special interest groups? TOPIX http://www.topix.net/forum/city/welch-wv/T47HBCSK-oK22ATJC7

4   *Ibid.*

5   Cate Malek, *Red/Blue Polarization*, July 2005, http://www.beyond-intractability.org/case_studies/Red_Blue.jsp citing Dean Paton, "The Race for Governor that Simply Won't End," *Christian Science Monitor*, November 22, 2004, p. 2.

6   David Broder, "Voters' Views Sharply Divided," *The Washington Post*, op-ed page, November 8, 2000.

7   Anne E. Kornblut, "Red or Blue — Which Are You? Take The Slate Quiz," *Slate*, July 14, 2004.

CHAPTER ONE - What 'Divide?': Our Phantom Political Conflicts

1   Morris P. Fiorina, with Samual J. Abrams, and Jeremy C. Pope, *Culture War: The Myth of a Polarized America*, Hoover Press, 2006.

2   Jonathan Rauch, "Bipolar Disorder: Is America Divided?" *The Atlantic Monthly*, Thursday, June 12, 2005.

3   The Pew Research Center for People and the Press; *Survey Reports* May 10, 2005 – *Beyond Red vs Blue, Republicans Divided About Role of Government – Democrats by Social and Personal Values*

4   Julia Preston and Marjorie Connelly, "Immigration Bill Provisions Gain Wide Support in Poll," *The New York Times Newsweek* poll, published May 25, 2007 http://www.nytimes.com/2007/05/25/us/25poll.html?ex=11815344 00&en=ea3e2cfb2af2c5a4&ei=5070

5   Dalia Sussman, "Poll Shows View of Iraq War Is Most Negative Since Start," *The New York Times*, May 25, 2007 http://www.nytimes. com/2007/05/25/washington/25view.html?ei=5070&en=f4a50860162e6ef3&ex= 1181534400&adxnnl=1&adxnnlx=1181401901-2/L/kFoqnNxtPxqhXzTuxg

6   Rauch, *op. cit.*

7   *Ibid.* Rauch calls this article 'impressive'; it was published in *The American Journal of Sociology* - "Have Americans' Social Attitudes Become more Polarized?"

8   Census Bureau voting records http://www.census.gov/population/ socdemo/voting/cps2004/tab02-1.xls

9   A. Lawrence Chickering, *Beyond Left and Right: Breaking the Political Stalemate*, 1993.

10   Cato's views on foreign policy, commonly viewed as on the right, are in fact hard to distinguish from the very left Institute for Policy Studies.

11   Examples include Clinton, Kerry, Cleland and half the Democratic Senators for, with Kennedy, Wellstone, Corzine and the other half against.

12   Several state Democratic Parties platforms back gay marriage, while all major potential Democratic Presidential candidates oppose it.

13   There are prominent pro- and anti-NAFTA Democrats.

CHAPTER TWO - Some Casualities of Partisan Politics

1   "United States: Uniform Crime Report, State Statistics from 1960 - 2006" http://www.disastercenter.com/crime/

2   *Going Straight - An Ex Convict/Psychologist tells us how and why: America's Crime Problem* http://www.going-straight.com/ACP.shtml

3   The video, which they have made and have shown all around the state, may be found at http://134.186.44.105/OPEC_Videos/sbreentryv22.asf)

4   *A Nation at Risk: The Imperative for Educational Reform*, published in 1983 by the US Department of Education's National Commission on Excellence in Education.

5   From the letter of transmittal of *A Nation at Risk*

6   See www.educategirls.org

7   Barbara Starfield, MD, "Medical Errors - A Leading Cause of Death," *The Journal of The American Medical Association (JAMA)*, Vol. 284, No 4, July 26, 2000. This article, written by Dr. Starfield, of the Johns Hopkins School of Hygiene and Public Health, shows that medical errors may be the third leading cause of death in the United States.

The report apparently shows there are 2,000 deaths/year from unnecessary surgery, 7000 deaths/year from medication errors in hospitals, 20,000 deaths/year from other errors in hospitals, 80,000 deaths/year from infections in hospitals, 106,000 deaths/year from non-error, adverse effects of medications – these total up to 225,000 deaths per year in the US from iatrogenic causes which ranks these deaths as the number three killer. Iatrogenic is a term used when a patient dies as a direct result of treatments by a physician, whether it is from misdiagnosis of the ailment or from adverse drug reactions used to treat the illness. (drug reactions are the most common cause). http://www.cancure.org/medical_errors.htm

8   Diana Saib, "Health Care For All - Speaking of Health Care," *Yes Magazine*, Fall 2006 http://www.yesmagazine.org/article.asp?ID=1508

9   *Ibid.*

10   "The U.S. Health Care System - Best in the world or just the most expensive?" Bureau of Education University of Maine http://dll.umaine.edu/ble/U.S.%20HCweb.pdf#search=%22 International%20Health%20Care%20Costs%20%3FComparisons%22

11   Walter M. Bortz, *Living Longer for Dummies*, 2001

12   See A. Lawrence Chickering, Emily Coleman, P. Edward Haley, and Emily Vargas-Baron, *Strategic Foreign Assistance: Civil Society in International Security,* Hoover Press, 2006 (Chapter Two).

13   De Soto's books are *The Other Path*, 1986; and *The Mystery of Capital*, 2003. An excellent summary of his work, including its impact in fighting terrorism in Peru, may be found in Chickering, et. al., *Strategic Foreign Assistance*, 2006.

17   One can read a year of issues of leading foreign policy journals – *Foreign Affairs, Foreign Policy, The National Interest, Orbis* – without seeing a single, positive article on civil society. Nor can one find discussion of its potential uses in these and other journals on any major foreign policy challenge: in the Middle East, in South Asia, in Sub-Saharan Africa – anywhere.

CHAPTER THREE - Transpartisan Capitalism I

1   Economist John Kenneth Galbraith's book, *The Affluent Society in the 1950s*, presented a liberals' powerful appeal for increasing commitment to the public good through the government, while the late Milton Friedman was the most famous intellectual promoting expansion of the private sector and for limiting the size of government. President Reagan's famous statement about "getting government off peoples' backs" also expressed the conservative commitment to reduce the size of government, while FDR affirmed liberals' belief in government when he advocated "a government strong enough to protect the interests of the people." Roosevelt's exact words were: "The only sure bulwark of continuing liberty is a government strong enough to protect the interests of the people. ..."

2   Recent examples include *Man v. the State*, *Shooter*, and the TV series *Prison Break*, among many others.

3   The liberal economist Charles Schultze laid out a general roadmap of issues on which market incentives and private interest could be used to promote the public good. See "The Public Use of Private Interest," *Harper's*, May 1977.

4   Chickering, *et., al., op. cit.* (Chapter Four)

5   There are many examples of traditional communities shifting toward "modern" empathy especially in the field of promoting girls' education in traditional, patriarchal cultures. One such experience that we know especially is that of Educate Girls Globally (EGG), working in the male-dominated state of Rajasthan in India. Working in two of the most backward and male-dominated districts in the state, Jalore and Pali, 47 out of the 50 schools in a pilot project fully mobilized to identify girls out of school and bring them back after eighteen months. The other three schools have achieved no progress, observers believe because the teachers assigned to lead the process did not take leadership. Similar results have been reported in Baluchistan and Northwest Frontier Province in Pakistan, in Upper Egypt, and many similar placed greatly influenced by fundamentalist Islam.

CHAPTER FOUR - National Security and 'the Long War'

1   *The Economist's* commentary on General Musharraf's anti-democratic actions in fall 2007 presents a good example of much recent comment on Musharraf and many other leaders in the region. Its lead editorial in the Nov 10-16, 2007, issue entitled "Time's up, Mr. Musharraf," concludes that Musharraf, once considered the only hope for democracy in Pakistan, is now "a big part of Pakistan's problem." The editorial begins with a pompous observation that although a military dictator, Musharraf "always seemed rather a decent sort." It then goes on to say that although he was well-intentioned in the beginning, he has failed because he ended up abandoning his democratic aspirations in favor of authoritarianism. The subtext of the editorial, as of much public comment, is that democracy is really a very sim-

ple proposition: you just have to do it. Well, no, it isn't. We are not well-served by simpleminded moralizing about complex issues.

2   Chickering, *et., al., op. cit.* (Chapter Two)

3   *Ibid.*

CHAPTER FIVE - Challenges of an Unconnected Society

1   At first *Brown v. Board of Education* made it unconstitutional for states to maintain racially-segregated schools, overturning the earlier court decision (*Plessy v. Ferguson*, in 1896) that segregated schools were fine as long as they were equal (the so-called "separate-but-equal" doctrine).

2   Just before the end of the past term, the Court issued a decision, written by Chief Justice John Roberts, that signaled a complete departure from more than half a century of jurisprudence on race. The case is called *Parents Involved in Community Schools v. Seattle School District No. 1*, and it addresses a legal challenge to two city school systems – Seattle's and Louisville's – for consciously trying to achieve racial integration in assigning students to particular schools. Nicholas Lemann, "Reversals," *The New Yorker*, July 30, 2007.

3   For a recent "ethnographic study" of Oak Park, see Temple University Professor Jay Ruby in an online report at http://astro.temple.edu/-ruby/opp. For background, see Carole Goodwin, *The Oak Park Strategy*, 1979.

4   Pat Riley, NBA Coach, p. 266-268, from his book, *The Winner Within*, 1994.

5   Juan Williams, *Enough: The Phony Leaders, Dead-End Movements, and Culture of Failure That Are Undermining Black America, and What We Can Do About It*, Crown Publishing Group, 2006.

6   Andrew Sullivan writes, in this context, about Harry Belafonte, 'Here's what Belafonte said: In the days of slavery, there were those slaves who lived on the plantation and there were those slaves that lived in the house. You got the privilege of living in the house if you served the master.' He added: 'Colin Powell's permitted to come into the house of the master. When Colin Powell dares to suggest something other than what the master wants to hear, he will be turned back out to pasture.' "The Bigotry of Belafonte," *Salon*, October 25, 2002. http://dir.salon.com/story/news/col/sullivan/2002/10/25/belafonte/

7   *Courting Justice, a History of Gay Rights Issues at the Supreme Court* by Joyce Murdoch and Deb Price, reports that there have been at least 22 gay law clerks at the court, and that in each of six consecutive terms in the 1980's, one of Justice Powell's four law clerks was gay. "Doubts still gnaw at Powell's ex-clerks about whether they could or should have done more to educate him," the book says.

8   Although political support for gay marriage is now limited, we do note that the California legislature did approve a gay marriage bill that the California governor vetoed (however, on procedural grounds). The Califor-

nia Supreme Court more recently affirmed gay marriage. Massachusetts continues to conduct gay marriages, and a number of churches offer marriage to gay couples.

PART III - THE TRANSPARTISAN IMPERATIVE

1   Add new information and organizing technologies rooted in the Internet to this constituency, and it becomes possible to imagine the — until now, nearly invisible — "also-rans" exerting a powerful, considered influence on the political direction of this country and the world. For example, in 2004, Joe Trippi and his associates used $2 million from the Howard Dean Democratic presidential primary campaign to raise $59 million, transforming not only the role of a little known former governor of a small Northeastern state from curiosity to front-runner, but also transforming political campaigning itself. Barack Obama raised more than $30 million in January 2008 alone, mostly on the Internet. Whatever else they do today, all serious candidates now campaign on the Internet.

Persuading five percent (6.5 million) of these 130 million extra-partisans annually to contribute $100 each to transpartisan political action funds, a task Trippi's team sees as technically doable, creates a $650 million dollar annual war chest. This amount exceeds the combined total spent by the Bush and Kerry campaigns in the 2004 U.S. presidential election. There are resources to support the transpartisan constituency.

CHAPTER SIX - A Call to Action

1   They write about this in Federalist Papers Nine and Ten — a two-part essay titled "The Union as a Safeguard Against Domestic Faction and Insurrection." These were two of 85 essays written in 1787 and 1788 to promote adoption of the newly drafted Constitution. In Federalist Papers Nine and Ten, Madison condemned the "dangerous vice... of faction," while Hamilton described the Constitution as an antidote to the damage caused by factions.

2   Doris Kearns Goodwin, *Team of Rivals: the Political Genius of Abraham Lincoln*, 2005.

CHAPTER SEVEN - Economics: Transpartisan Capitalism II

1   For a more complete discussion of this point, see A. Lawrence Chickering, *Beyond Left and Right*, 1993.

2   In his book *Making Schools Work*, William Ouchi, Professor of Business Administration at UCLA, analyzes three highly functioning school districts — Edmonton, Canada; Seattle, WA; and Houston, TX — which decentralize considerable authority to individual schools. He presents considerable evidence that this is the single most important reform that could strengthen public schools.

3   An easy way to find a list of examples of successful public schools informally operating like charter schools is to look at a list of the winners of the state contests run by the National Association for School Administrators and their state affiliates for outstanding principals. The awards are given annually

in each state, and then a national winner is selected by the National Association for the country. Jim Dierke won the award as the outstanding principal of a middle school in 2007, and he was selected the outstanding principal in the country in 2008.

4   Voters have been able to vote on several statewide voucher initiatives in California. Each time teachers' unions have mobilized and spent massive amounts of money and have defeated them by wide margins. Money spent in favor of vouchers seems to make no difference. In the last statewide initiative, in 2000, a Silicon Valley venture capitalist put up nearly $30 million in support of the initiative, and voters defeated it by a 71–29 margin.

5   The Copenhagen Consensus was a project organized by the Danish political scientist Bjorn Lomborg, which recruited eight famous economists to spend a mythical $50 billion on twenty-eight internal economic and social challenges. They allocated the most money to AIDS ($27 billion), and climate change was one of their lowest priorities.

CHAPTER EIGHT - Recruiting Citizens as Partners for National Security and Foreign Policy

1   Chickering, *et., al., op. cit.* (Chapter Five)

2   *Ibid.* (Chapter Six)

3   For an introduction to the world of Civic Society and CSOs see http://web.worldbank.org/WBSITE/EXTERNAL/TOPICS/CSO/0,,contentMDK:21426 033~pagePK:220503~piPK:220476~theSitePK:228717,00.html

4   An example is The Amy Biehl Foundation, which is a quintessential transpartisan undertaking whose story conveys the heart of the transpartisan impulse. The foundation was established to commemorate the life of Amy Biehl, a 26-year-old Stanford University student and Fulbright Scholar, who was murdered on the evening of Aug. 25, 1993, in Gugulethu township outside of Cape Town, South Africa. Years later, the four youths convicted of murdering her and given prison sentences of eighteen years applied for amnesty from South Africa's Truth and Reconciliation Commission (TRC), which was created by Nelson Mandela's Government of National Unity in 1995 to allow South Africans to come to terms with their extremely troubled past. In a decision the family endorsed, the TRC pardoned Biehl's killers in 1998 and released them from prison after serving four years. At the hearings, the Biehls shook hands with their daughter's killers, and Peter Biehl addressed the Commission hearings in the following words: "The most important vehicle of reconciliation is open and honest dialogue... we are here to reconcile a human life which was taken without an opportunity for dialogue. When we are finished with this process we must move forward with linked arms." The Biehls said they believe their daughter would have supported the Commission's decision to grant amnesty. Two of the convicted murderers now work for the foundation. http://www.myhero.com/myhero/hero.asp?hero=a_biehl

CHAPTER NINE - Re-engaging Society: Race, Gays, Religion, and Spirituality

1   Robert Putnam reached identical conclusions in his long-term study of Italy. See Robert Lonardi, Raffaella Y. Nanetti, and Robert Putnam, *Making Democracy Work*, 1993.

2   Released Feb. 25 2008 by The Pew Forum on Religion & Public Life

3   http://religions.pewforum.org/reports

CHAPTER TEN - Transpartisan: Past, Present and Future

1   http://www.apttax.com/news.php

2   http://www.apttax.com/WisconsinStateJournal.doc

3   http://www.apttax.com/NYTimesArticle.doc

4   http://www.chaordic.org/

5   http://www.fastcompany.com/magazine/05/deehock.html

6   http://www.abrahampath.org/about.php?lang=en

7   http://www.abrahampath.org/downloads/cincinnati.pdf
The Abraham Path website has detailed instructions on how to hold a local event

8   "The Gang of 14" was a term coined to describe the bipartisan group of moderate senators in the 109th United State Congress who successfully negotiated a compromise in the spring of 2005 to avoid the deployment of the so-called nuclear option (or constitutional option) over an organized use of the filibuster by Senate Democrats to prevent the confirmation of conservative appellate court candidates nominated by President George W. Bush. http://en.wikipedia.org/wiki/Gang_of_14

CHAPTER ELEVEN - An Awakened America

1   http://www.nytimes.com/2008/02/28/opinion/28mike.html?hp

2   Louis Menand, *The Metaphysical Club: A Story of Ideas in America,*

CONCLUSION

1   For a full discussion of this point, see A. Lawrence Chickering, ed., *Public Employee Unions: The Crisis in Public Sector Labor Relations* (1977), especially the chapters by Harvey Mansfield, Jr., and Robert Nisbet.

Acknowledgements

As a "conservative" and a "liberal", we came to our transpartisan position by very different routes. The logic of our convergence is pretty simple, and it may be imagined from our argument about the limited value of the words "conservative" and "liberal" to describe real things — people and issues. We have argued that our four-part matrix, separating left and right into freedom and order components (freedom-left, order-left, freedom-right, and order-right) much better describes both issues and people in our political process. We believe each of the positions represents part of the truth, and the challenge, therefore, is to integrate them. The result will not only bring people together who are now lost in hopeless conflict; it will also help formulate strategies for solving problems that now seem beyond solution.

In tracing our intellectual paths, we came to the reluctant conclusion that our intellectual debts are too vast and our time too limited to do them justice. Therefore, rather than try separately to recognize every person who has influenced us over many years, we decided to focus our thanks on two influences that played special roles for each of us. Our special thanks follow.

CHICKERING: I want to express my gratitude to William F. Buckley, Jr., and Milton Friedman, my two skiing buddies, who over nineteen years of skiing together and beyond, gave me unparalleled opportunities to explore every imaginable issue examined here. I was still working on the transpartisan vision we have presented here and therefore could not articulate it all before they died — Milton in late 2006, and Bill in early 2008. Nevertheless, I listened with great care in many conversations to their thoughts on the principal issues explored here. Our discussions were especially interesting on the tensions between the freedom and order components of conservative thought, and sometimes they were on opposite sides of the argument. Both were powerful influences in my contribution to this essay.

TURNER: I express *my* gratitude to two Washington, DC, neighbors: Esther Peterson, who, for my first thirty years in Washington, gave me first-hand access to the labor, feminist, and civil rights movements, whose traditions were first taught to me by my parents; and Arthur J. Goldberg, for whom my son worked as an assistant and who, in the last decade of his life, let me see how a restless activist might find even the Supreme Court of the United States confining. From both of them I gathered vital insights into activist living, cooperative innovation, and the American experience that shaped my thinking as presented in this book.

We would like to express special thanks to John Marks, founder and President of Search for Common Ground, who introduced us at a party he gave in Washington, DC, for Lawry's 1993 book, *Beyond Left and Right*. The introduction led to a friendship and dialogue that produced this essay and is still continuing in development of future projects together.

In terms of acknowledgements for help on the book, we want to thank the following for reading parts or all of the manuscript, for commenting on it, and/or for other kinds of help on our intellectual vision: Tom Atlee, Todd Barrett, Larry Biehl, Stephen P. Cohen, James Dierke, Edward Haley, Helen Jepsen, Rachael Kessler, Betsy Lehrfeld, Joseph McCormick, John Steiner, Serena Ventura, and Jeff Weinglass.

We want to thank The da Vinci Society and da Vinci Press for seeing the importance of the book and especially the importance of publishing it quickly, during the extraordinary 2008 Presidential campaign. In the normal publishing timetable, publishers talked about publishing the book in spring 2009. The advent of new technologies and especially the Internet made it possible for da Vinci, committed to promoting transpartisan ideas, to accept, edit and publish the book in about ten weeks. Specifically, we want to thank Larry Biehl, founder of da Vinci, for his support in a variety of ways, including editing the manuscript (twice!), Todd Barrett, Michele Casteel, Orion Casteel, Helen Jepsen, Dan Kass, Warner Henry, Ed Levy, and Felina Mohammed.

Finally, we want to thank our many colleagues in Reuniting America, representing all sectors in our four-part political matrix, who have participated in numerous workshops, conferences, and discussions that helped frame our perspective and positions on particular issues. These individuals have leadership and senior positions in some of the most famous conservative and liberal advocacy groups in America, with a combined membership exceeding 30 million people.

In particular, we express special thanks to Joseph McCormick and Pat Spino, founders of Reuniting America, who had the vision to create this extraordinary organization and to bring us together. Among those who played special leadership roles, we need to mention Ana Micka and Michael Ostrolenk, co-directors, and Mark Gerzon, John Steiner, and Bill Ury. We also want to thank the following for their participation as members of the National Steering Committee, as National Advisors, or as participants in major conferences: Gary Aldrich, Jim Babka, Bob Barr, Tom Beach, Joan Blades, Michelle Bernard, Laura Chasin, Roberta Combs, Robert Fersh, Carl Fillichio, Maggie Fox, Brenda Girton-Mitchell, Joe Goldman, Vice President Al Gore, Cheryl Graeve, Susan Hackley, Sandy Heierbacher, Scott Heiferman, Irma Herrera, Barbara Hubbard, Ethan Leib, Dave Keating, David Keene, Carolyn Lukensmeyer, Patrice McDermott,

Marian Moore, Grover Norquist, Samah Norquist, Carah Ong, Trita Parsi, Susan Partnow, Chellie Pingree, Julie Ristau, Vicki Robin, John Rother, Mark Satin, Rick Shelby, Ginny Sloan, Fred Smith, Robert Spanogle, Betsy Taylor, Bill Thompson, Michael Toms, Leif Utne, William Westmiller, Donna Wiesner, Shirley Wilcher, and Ahmed Younis.

Without their inspiration and support, we could not have written this book.

A. LAWRENCE CHICKERING   **JAMES S. TURNER**
San Francisco, California   *Washington, DC*

A. LAWRENCE CHICKERING

A. Lawrence Chickering is a political and social entrepreneur and writer whose work has focused on empowering citizens to play an increased role in public institutions from government schools to foreign policy.

He began his career in public policy working for William F. Buckley, Jr., at *National Review*, the magazine Buckley founded. They remained close friends until Buckley's death in 2008.

Chickering has founded or co-founded several organizations that promote reforms in the United States and other countries that appeal to both conservatives and liberals. Throughout his work is a strong emphasis on conflict resolution. His organization, Educate Girls Globally (EGG), which works in India, has developed a process that effects cultural transformation not only in traditional communities, but also in government bureaucratic cultures.

In 1985, he co-founded the International Center for Economic Growth, which, in a ten-year period, helped promote major reforms in more than fifty countries. More recently, he has been a co-founder of Reuniting America, a citizen organization bringing together officials of major conservative and liberal organizations in the U.S.

His book *Beyond Left and Right* (1993) drew wide praise across the U.S. political spectrum, and his co-authored 2006 book *Strategic Foreign Assistance: Civil Society in International Security* is part of a new (post 9/11) way of thinking about foreign policy.

He is currently working on two new books, both with co-authors. One is a transpartisan strategy for reforming U.S. foreign policy, and the other is a transpartisan strategy for reforming U.S. public schools.

Mr. Chickering is a graduate of Stanford University and the Yale Law School. He lives in San Francisco with his wife and son.

JAMES S. TURNER

James S. Turner Esq., original Nader's Raider and partner in the Washington, DC, law firm of Swankin & Turner (founded in 1973), wrote the *"Chemical Feast: The Nader Report on Food Protection at the Food and Drug Administration,"* which *Time Magazine* said, "... may well be the most devastating critique of a U.S. Government Agency ever issued."

He served as consumer affairs consultant to Democratic Governor John Gilligan of Ohio, special counsel to the U.S. Senate Select Committee on Nutrition and Human Needs chaired by Senator George McGovern (D-SD), and the Government Operations Sub-committee on Government Research led by Senator Abraham Ribicoff (D-Conn).

Turner successfully opposed a 1975 Federal Trade Commission proposed ban of the word "organic;" helped lobby the Organic Food Production Act of 1990 through Congress and helped stop a 1999 Department of Agriculture effort to weaken organic food standards. His legal team got FDA to approve acupuncture needles. He currently serves as board chair of Citizens for Health and hosts a weekly one hour internet inter-view program, "Of Consuming Interest," on the Progressive Radio Network.

Turner served as a gunnery and nuclear weapons handling officer on U.S. Navy ships from 1962-1966.

He graduated from Ohio State University with a BA in history and political science in 1962, where he was a leader in the Ohio State Free Speech Movement, and then from Ohio State University Moritz College of Law in 1969, where he was co-director of the Columbus Ohio Vietnam Summer anti-Vietnam War group, and an editor of the *Law and Civil Rights Bulletin*.

Born in Columbus and raised in Cleveland, Ohio, he now lives in Washington, DC, with his partner, Betsy E. Lehrfeld.

STEPHEN P. COHEN

Stephen P. Cohen, a psychologist by training, has exemplified transpartisan values throughout his three-decade career.

A major influence in several of the most important and successful Middle East peace initiatives, he created the first secret official negotiations between Israel and the PLO, years before the Oslo peace process. He served as confidant of both Israel's Foreign Minister Moshe Dayan and Egypt's President Anwar Sadat and set up the first meetings between Shimon Peres and Sadat and between Yitzhak Rabin, Peres and Abba Eban and the leaders of Egypt's National Democratic Party.

Dr. Cohen has a long history of transcending the limitations of particular partisan views. His life is a testament to the importance of trust in human affairs.

More advance praise for

VOICE OF THE PEOPLE

"I've spent most of my 40 years in politics on the Right because of my belief in limited government. However, I have recently been discovering that the old labels of left/right, liberal/conservative no longer apply. Common ground is being found through left/right coalitions on personal privacy issues, free market solutions to poverty, and even foreign policy. Read *Voice of the People* to learn how such integration can work"

— TOM DEWEESE
President, American Policy Center

"This book challenges our traditional, political boundaries and stereotypes and offers a road map to usher in a new era for citizen creativity and effectiveness. Kudos to Turner and Chickering for a new sound system for the voice of the people."

— ROBERT GASS, *Leadership coach, facilitator,*
and expert on Organizational Transformation

"*Voice of the People* provides a timely wake-up to all of us who are working to transform and humanize our public institutions. The authors help us go beyond our stereotypes about "the other side" to see the rich tensions that live in each side and connect us in common concern for a caring democracy. As an educator working to give students tools for crossing the divides, I was moved by the role they see for citizen engagement to rebuild trust and meaningful connection in our public life and offer creative solutions to some of our most pressing challenges."

— RACHAEL KESSLER
Founder, director The Passageworks Institute; author,
"The Soul of Education: Helping Students find Connection,
Compassion, and Character at School"

"In *Voice of the People*, Chickering and Turner have recognized the public's disgust with partisan polarization and winner take all politics and the cost to the country. For all Americans who want to get beyond the labels, work from deeply held values and join hands to partner on solving the major social and economic issues of our day, *Voice of the People* is a breath of fresh air."

– **CAROLYN J. LUKENSMEYER**
President and founder, AmericaSpeaks

"In *Voice of the People*, Lawry Chickering and Jim Turner have made a vital contribution to a growing movement in America politics. It is a movement rooted in the wisdom of *E Pluribus Unum* – from many, one.   They eloquently advance the notion of citizens as partners with government, arguing that average Americans are a vast untapped resource seeking a means to contribute to economic and social progress. Millions of people from all points of view – left, right, and center – are waking up, linking up and seeking guidance about how to re-engage. Now they have a manifesto."

– **JOSEPH MCCORMICK**
Co-founder and chairman, Reuniting America

"*Voice of the People* is visionary for outlining steps to move us towards the next stage of political engagement… and it might actually work. Chickering and Turner have outlined real world solutions in the midst of a conceptual paradigm shift. As I read, I wanted to engage the authors in dialogue. More importantly, I can't wait to gather community members to begin a transpartisan dialogue about our local issues."

– **DEBILYN MOLINEAUX**
Community Activist, Fresno, CA;
Political Leadership Coach

"Chickering and Turner turn our thinking upside down, challenging readers to think about issues from public school reform to foreign policy in new ways. At the heart of their analysis is a profound critique of mechanistic thinking that has dominated Western thought for at least three centuries. They present a powerful case for a new humanistic and spiritual politics based on empowering citizens both inside and outside the government. At a time when most people feel only despair about American politics, this book brings a strong source of new hope."

– MICHAEL MURPHY
Founder, Esalen Institute; author,
"The Future of the Body" and "Golf and the Kingdom"

"Turner and Chickering are not saying the right is wrong or the left is right, but that both left and right offer only partial ways of understanding and sustainably dealing with complex issues. The key to solving this conundrum is to transcend the limits of each and integrate their strengths. They also recognize that the so-called left and right do not include a new large "post-partisan" demographic which is now emerging and has yet to find a political home that truly expresses its interests.   This illuminating book also offers a fresh architecture and compelling interpersonal processes for dealing with the various, thorny challenges – political, economic, social, cultural, and spiritual – that we face as a nation."

– MICHAEL D. OSTROLENK
President, American Conservative Defense Alliance;
Chair, The Liberty Coalition

"Whatever happened to 'We the People'? Whatever happened to the democratic side of our Democratic Republic? ***Voice of the People: The Transpartisan Imperative in American Life*** offers a series of simple, stunning, and profound answers to these important and timely questions. ***Voice of the People*** suggests a humanizing framework for bringing our democracy back to the American people and for bringing bold, out-of-the-box ideas into our national policy debates."

– JOHN STEINER
Co-founder, The National Commons;
Chair, The Transpartisan Center

"A highly constructive book—a powerful antidote to the insidious poison of partisan hatred that undermines the discussion and implementation of constructive solutions to our nation's problems."

– MICHAEL STRONG
*CEO, FLOW, a non-profit dedicated to
"Liberating the Entrepreneurial Spirit for Good"*

"Two centuries ago, George Washington warned us of the perils of partisanship. Today we have the opportunity to heed his sage advice and create a new forem of 'transpartisan' politics that empowers citizens and respects differences as it distills unity out of diversity. This revolutionary and provocative essay shows us how. Read it at your own risk!"

– WILLIAM URY
*Co-author, "Getting to Yes"; author,
"The Third Side" and "The Power of a Positive No"*

"As America's ruling establishment drives us ever downward to the mutual hatreds of partisan orthodoxies, Lawry Chickering and Jim Turner offer us a lifeline. They understand how our deep identity – shaped by a unique American religious nationalism – is today at risk. They witness the damage of conflicts within ourselves, and they testify to the heartfelt desire of ordinary Americans to reunite and feel together again. If anything, they are a sign – hopefully one of many! – that the people, aware of where we stand and what is at stake, can come together once more to renew American identity."

– MICHAEL VLAHOS
*Director, Center for the Study of Foreign Affairs,
U.S. Department of State, 1988-1991
Author "Fighting Identity" (forthcoming)*

"*Voice of the People* provides hope that the era of divisive politics in America may finally be ending. Chickering and Turner invite us to think and talk and work together to confront our challenges. They provide both a way out of our polarization and a way in for many people to make a real contribution to the common good."

– JEFF WEISSGLASS
Advisory Board Chair, The Project on Civic Reflection
Core Team Member, The Transpartisan Center

"*Voice of the People* is an important, timely, often profound call for a more integral politics, in theory and in action. It is the first step toward the creation of a political culture that heals rather than hurts, integrates rather than fragments, and unites rather than divides. If its recommendations were actually put into action, we would see nothing less than a transformation of humanity itself."

– KEN WILBER
Philosopher; author, "The Integral Vision"

"*Voice of the People: The Transpartisan Imperative in American Life* provides real substance to the politics of hope and to reviving the dream of democracy we've carried with us from the days of our founders. Lawry Chickering and Jim Turner have given us a breathtakingly simple and doable blueprint for reclaiming our political system."

– DONNA ZAJONC
Former Oregon state representative; author,
"The Politics of Hope: Reviving the Dream of Democracy"